The Intelligence of Evil or the Lucidity Pact

The Intelligence of Evil
or the Lucidity Pact

Jean Baudrillard

Translated by Chris Turner

BERG

Oxford • New York

English Edition
First published in 2005 by
Berg
Editorial offices:
1st Floor, Angel Court, 81 St Clements Street, Oxford, OX4 1AW, UK
175 Fifth Avenue, New York, NY 10010, USA

First published in France, 2004 by Editions Galilée
© Galilée, 2004, *Le Pacte de lucidité ou l'intelligence du Mal*

Introduction and English translation © Chris Turner 2005

This work is published with the support of the French Ministry of Culture –
Centre National du Livre

ıı institut français

This book is supported by the French Ministry for Foreign Affairs as part of the Burgess
Programme headed for the French Embassy in London by the Institut Français du Royaume-Uni

Berg is the imprint of Oxford International Publishers Ltd.

Library of Congress Cataloguing-in-Publication Data

Baudrillard, Jean.
    [Pacte de lucidité ou l'intelligence du Mal. English]
    The intelligence of evil or the lucidity pact / Jean Baudrillard ; translated by
Chris Turner.— English ed.
    p. cm.
    Includes index.
    ISBN 1-84520-327-5 (cloth) — ISBN 1-84520-334-8 (pbk.)
  1. Reality. 2. Good and evil. I. Title.

    B2430.B33973P3313 2005
    194—dc22

                                 2005017087

British Library Cataloguing-in-Publication Data

A catalogue record for this book is available from the British Library.

ISBN-13 978 1 84520 327 6 (Cloth)
          978 1 84520 334 4 (Paper)

ISBN-10 1 84520 327 5 (Cloth)
          1 84520 334 8 (Paper)

Typeset by JS Typesetting, Porthcawl, Mid Glamorgan
Printed in the United Kingdom by Biddles Ltd, King's Lynn

www.bergpublishers.com

Contents

We accept the real so readily only because we sense that reality does not exist.

Jorge Luis Borges

Last night I had a dream about reality.
It was such a relief to wake up.

Stanislaw J. Lec

The Intelligence of Evil
An Introduction

CHRIS TURNER

> The role of the translator is not to bring out, by a commentary, the author's intentions and connotations...

Claude Fages[1]

> A revolutionary age is an age of action; ours is the age of advertisement and publicity. Nothing ever happens but there is immediate publicity everywhere.

Søren Kierkegaard[2]

Jean Baudrillard was born in Reims in 1929. Among his earliest published writings were reviews of literature for *Les Temps modernes* at a time when he was still teaching German at a provincial *lycée* and translating the works, among others, of Peter Weiss, Bertolt Brecht and Wilhelm Mühlmann. In the 1960s he made the transition to sociology, largely under the guidance of Henri Lefebvre, and began to teach the subject

1. 'Note du traducteur' in José Saramago, *L'année de la mort de Ricardo Reis* (Paris: Seuil, 1988), p. 9.
2. *The Present Age*. Translated and with an Introduction by Alexander Du. (London: Collins, 1962), p. 36.

in October 1966 at the (small, but very radical) University of Nanterre.[3] In his teaching at that time, he drew, he tells us, almost exclusively on four books: Artaud's *Le théâtre de la cruauté*, *The Accursed Share* by Georges Bataille, Marcel Mauss's *Essay on the Gift* and *La Monnaie vivante* by Pierre Klossowski, translator of, and commentator on, Nietzsche.[4] As regards other, perhaps even more ingrained, influences, Baudrillard speaks freely of his early Nietzscheanism and his encounter during his schooldays with Jarry's pataphysics.

Baudrillard's first period as a social theorist began with an analysis of the world of everyday objects and, by extension, of advertising and the media, in such works as *The System of Objects* (1968), *The Consumer Society* (1970) and *For a Critique of the Political Economy of the Sign* (1972).[5] These were the years of the journal *Utopie*, to which he made many contributions over the period 1967–78, publishing there for the first time chapters from *The Mirror of Production*, his theoretical rejection of Marxism as productivism. This work, which appeared in book form later in 1973, and which takes up in its critical sweep not only Marxism, but the 'textual productivity' of *Tel Quel* and Deleuze/Guattari's machinic productivity of the unconscious, 'moves decisively to change the basis of his position away from that of a traditional concept of class struggle to that of opposing the symbolic order to the semiotic (or simulation)

3. Nanterre was the birthplace of the 'mouvement du 22 mars', which played a prominent role in the events of May 1968. Baudrillard left Nanterre in 1986, at a point when it had been definitively 'normalized', and spent the latter part of his teaching career at Paris-IX Dauphine. The offer of the move to Paris-IX apparently came from Marc Guillaume.
4. *Fragments*. Translated by Chris Turner (London: Routledge, 2004), p. 39.
5. Though it should be said that *The Consumer Society* was written to a commission from a publisher and Baudrillard does not see it as representative of his intellectual trajectory at the time.

order constituent of contemporary Western culture.'[6] In particular, Baudrillard mounts an 'anthropological' challenge to Marx's championing of use-value against exchange-value, a position based ultimately on the assumption that use-values merely subserve human needs aculturally and transparently.[7]

In *Symbolic Exchange and Death* (1976), which opens with the assertion that 'There is no longer any symbolic exchange, as organizing form, at the level of modern social formations',[8] Baudrillard pitches his tent firmly on the ground of Mauss's theory of gift-exchange and Bataille's 'general economy' (and also Saussure's writings on anagrams) and begins in earnest the elaboration of the radical anthropology on which his analyses will draw most centrally over the coming years.[9] Here he develops his theory of the three orders of simulacra,[10] arguing, in particular, that we have passed out of the industrial era, in which production was the dominant pattern, into a code-governed phase where the dominant

6. Mike Gane, *Jean Baudrillard: In Radical Uncertainty*, p. 13.
7. Thinkers within the world of anthropology were engaged on similar critiques at this same time, though rarely with an equal degree of radicalism. See, for example, Marshall Sahlins, *Culture and Practical Reason* (Chicago and London: University of Chicago Press, 1976).
8. *L'échange symbolique et la mort* (Paris: Gallimard, 1976), p. 9. My translation.
9. See Georges Bataille, *The Accursed Share: An Essay on General Economy*. Translated by Robert Hurley (New York: Zone Books, 1991); Marcel Mauss, *The Gift: The Form and Reason for Exchange in Archaic Societies*. Translated by W. D. Halls (London: Routledge, 1990). Some have criticized Baudrillard's reliance on an anthropological critique as representing a nostalgic dimension in his work (e.g. Julian Pefanis, *Heterology and the Postmodern* [Durham, NC and London: Duke University Press, 1991], p. 112), but Baudrillard is always keen to dispel such a reading. In conversation with Maria Elena Ramos at Caracas in 1994, he describes his position as representing 'la nostalgia di une cultura non primitiva, sino radical' ('nostalgia for a culture not primitive, but radical').
10. *L'échange symbolique et la mort*, p. 77.

schema is *simulation*. Simulation is, as he puts it elsewhere, the replacement of the world with a kind of substitute universe, a counter-world of signs. What is alien to it – and essential to the symbolic order – is *la réversibilité* (the reversibility/ revertibility) of signs, particularly of life and death, proper to symbolic exchange. Within *réversibilité* is understood the possibility of actual *ré-version* – reversion/reverting/turnabout – and beneath it there are echoes of the act of *re-verser*.[11] paying back, making the counter-gift.

In an article entitled 'La prise d'otage' (Hostage taking), also published in *Utopie*[12] and incorporated with minor changes into *Symbolic Exchange and Death*, the political import of this understanding of the symbolic is brought out: 'It is impossible to destroy the system by a contradiction-based logic or by reversing the balance of forces – in short, by a direct, dialectical revolution affecting the economic or political infrastructure. Everything that produces contradiction or a balance of forces or energy in general merely feeds back into the system and drives it on.'[13] Hence,

> the worst error, the one committed by all our revolutionary strategists, is to think they can put an end to the system on the *real* plane: that is ... the imaginary the system itself imposes on them, a system that lives and survives only by getting those who attack it to fight on the terrain of reality, a ground that is always its own.[14]

---

11. V*erser* being understood here in the very basic sense of handing over, as in the expression '*verser une somme*'.
12. In March–April 1976.
13. Jean Baudrillard, *Le ludique et le policier et autres textes parus dans Utopie [1967/78]* (Paris: Sens & Tonka, 2001), p. 335.
14. Ibid., p. 336.

Realism' is no kind of radicalism at all: the only solution is 'to challenge the system with a gift to which it cannot reply – except by its own death and collapse'.[15] Though the overt pretext for this piece is a terrorist act – and we may consider this, too, as significant – Baudrillard's political thinking in this period is dominated, like that of many around him, by the events of 1968 and their aftermath.[16]

Baudrillard's work of the late 1970s and early 1980s spells out the implications of his vision for the various domains of social theory with which he was then engaged (at least nominally) in his professional life: sexuality and the family, the social sphere (where the 'crisis' of the welfare state had emerged as a key problem) and politics.[17] In *A l'ombre des majorités silencieuses ... ou la fin du social* (in a magnificently suicidal gesture for a practising sociologist), he offers at least four – not entirely compatible – lines of reasoning to support the argument that '*le social*' is no longer (or never was) a pertinent category for study: there is no 'social', there are only networks of symbolic obligations, which are not social relations since the constraint they impose does not assume contractual form. And, crucially, he also argues there that our modern western societies, having existed up to then on a basis of 'expansion and explosion at all levels', were on the point of implosion, a process heralded by the prevalence of terrorism in its radical non-representativeness and by the –

15. Ibid., p. 337.
16. Baudrillard tells an interviewer, 'May '68 was an illogical event, irreducible to simulation, one which had no status other than that of coming from someplace else – a kind of pure object or event', and one senses here the traces of a kind of 'primal scene'.
17. He was at this time team-teaching a seminar at Nanterre with Jacques Donzelot, who gives a fine account of their collaboration – and the differences between them – in 'Patasociologie à l'université de Nanterre', *L'Herne: Jean Baudrillard*

near-heroic – inertia and non-socialization of the symbolically astute masses ('They know there is no liberation and that a system is abolished only by pushing it into hyperlogic...'[18]). With *De la séduction* of 1979 a further key term takes its place among the battery of concepts that structure Baudrillard's symbolic order: 'With the decline of psychoanalysis and sexuality as strong structures,' he writes, 'one may catch a glimpse of another, parallel universe..., a universe that can no longer be interpreted in terms of psychic or psychological relations, nor those of repression and the unconscious, but must be interpreted in the terms of play, challenges, duels, the strategy of appearances – that is, in the terms of *seduction*.'[19] And with this comes a recognition of what Baudrillard calls 'the supremacy of the object', a recognition that it is not the subject and its desire, but the object and its seduction that orders the world.[20]

---

18. *In the Shadow of the Silent Majorities.* Translated by Paul Foss, John Johnston and Paul Patton (New York: Semiotext(e), 1983), p. 46.

19. *Seduction.* Translated by Brian Singer (London and Basingstoke: Macmillan Education, 1990), p. 7. My emphasis. Needless to say, this is a thoroughly post-structuralist position. The passage continues: 'A universe that can no longer be interpreted in terms of structures and diacritical oppositions, but implies a seductive reversibility.' Similarly, in *La fin du social*, Baudrillard writes: 'The challenge [*le défi*] is not a dialectic, nor a confrontation between respective poles, or terms, in a full structure [*une structure pleine*]. It is a process of *extermination* of the structural position of each *term*, of the subject position of each of the antagonists, and in particular of the one who issues the challenge.' *In the Shadow of the Silent Majorities*, p. 69 (translation modified).

20. *Les stratégies fatales* (Paris: Grasset, 1983), p. 172. This is a radical, unprecedented shift, engendering what one commentator has called a 'post-metaphysical tension' in Baudrillard's writings 'De subjectobject relatie wordt dus niet zozeer opgelost, als wel omgekeerd, waardoor een postmetafysische spanning wordt gecreëerd...' Henk Oosterling. 'Filosofie als schijnbeweging. Metafoor, metamorfose en ironie in het latere Werk van Jean Baudrillard', *Lier en Boog*, 7, 1, (1990) p. 37.

As seduction moves to the fore (or at least *la séduction*, which is not quite semantically equivalent to its English cognate), so, in the spiralling movement of Baudrillard's thought, the concept of production comes into focus once again and mutates subtly into its underlying, etymological sense of leading forward (*pro-ducere*), of bringing into the open, exposing and over-exposing. Since what is over-exposed is, of course, obscene, the 'poetics' of the symbolic order can be seen now virtually to volunteer the opposition between seduction and scene, on the one hand, production and the obscene, on the other. This spiralling play between concepts is a characteristic and durable feature of Baudrillard's *écriture:* as, in his later work, he increasingly 'withdraws' himself as active subject and goes over, as he puts it, to the side of the object, this sense of a poetic (and often ironic) dynamic within language itself underwrites the authenticity of the symbolic order and its various 'forms', which can thereby be seen also to preserve a secret, to guard a mystery.[21] And this repeats at another level the idea that the 'symbolic', the order of challenge, seduction and 'play', is not only what is repressed in modern western cultures, but also what is most resistant within them and is, in a sense, a hidden key to their functioning.[22] What

21. One aspect of which is that canonic sociological explanations entirely miss the point: 'Deep down, things have never functioned socially, but symbolically, magically, irrationally, etc.' *In the Shadow of the Silent Majorities*, p. 68 (translation modified). Pietro Bellasi pointed long ago to the 'ingrained poetic quality' of Baudrillard's theoretical writings: 'se non è poesia, c'è la grana profonda e segreta della poesia'. 'Introduzione' in Jean Baudrillard, *Dimenticare Foucault* (Bologna: Cappelli editore, 1977), p. 33.
22. There is also something resistant, reversible and almost initiatory in Baudrillard's terminology itself: 'symbolic exchange' describes an order in which there is no exchange; '*les stratégies fatales*' are 'not really strategies' and the so-called 'perfect crime' is in actual fact a crime *of* perfection.

we also see here, too, is a characteristic recourse to a *third term* that stands outside the apparently given dichotomy of production/destruction: 'seduction' is, as it were, the option from left field (Baudrillard also says it is the 'feminine' one, but that is another matter), the term that comes from outside the structure – from 'elsewhere'.

From this period onward, Baudrillard's understanding of the *pro-duction* of the world becomes increasingly radical. There is a sense not just that all hope of an alternative social project has 'imploded', not merely that 'all potential modes of expression' have been absorbed into 'that of advertising',[23] but that, with the merciless advance of simulation, a reality is being produced that is extreme in itself, extreme in the absence of critical distance it grants us, in the all-enveloping nature of its short-circuited, real-time, asphyxiating immediacy. At the same time, where once it was capital that caused all that was solid to melt into air, now a process of the 'destructuration of every referential, of every human objective' – the process Baudrillard calls the 'deterrence ... of every principle'[24] – has turned around against power, capitalist or other, and reduced every institutional reality to simulation (and hyperreality: things do not disappear by their determinate negation, but by being driven on to this 'hyper' level). This is the world of the 'beyond', of the 'after': *The Transparency of Evil* (1993) opens with a piece entitled 'After the Orgy', the orgy in question being 'the moment when modernity exploded upon us, the moment of liberation in every sphere'.[25] In conversation

---

23. *Simulacra and Simulation.* Translated by Shela Faria Glaser (Ann Arbor: University of Michigan Press, 1994), p. 87 (translation modified).
24. Ibid., p. 22.
25. *The Transparency of Evil.* Translated by James Benedict (London: Verso, 1993), p. 3.

with the Russian artist Boris Groys in 1995, Baudrillard says: 'What we have to deal with now is the fact that our entire culture has, through simulation, the media etc., gone over into something else, into a space beyond the end.' And he adds, 'Things have no origin any longer and no end, they cannot develop logically or dialectically any more, but only chaotically or randomly. They are becoming 'extreme' in the literal sense – *ex terminis*: they are beyond the limits.'[26] A radical implosion has taken place and we have survived 'beyond the end', beyond a situation that could be grasped by our earlier categories of rational or dialectical thought. The course of the world is now dominated by a grandiose programme of total production which itself supplants the world, *realizes* it in the sense of turning it wholly into known, rationally structured reality, seeks to produce a *total* simulation, a virtual reality that aspires to obliterate entirely Baudrillard's realm of symbolic exchange.[27]

As the joint assault on the symbolic order by *l'information* and *l'informatique* escalates and mere 'simulation' (the state in

26. From the website of the Zentrum für Kunst und Medientechnologie on the occasion of the presentation of the Siemens Media Prize of 1995 (*http://on1.zkm. de/zkm/stories/storyReader$1089*). Note the '*ex terminis*' here, which lays the ground for a linkage of this excess with the exterminatory mode, just as Baudrillard's play on *croissance* and *excroissance* (growth and excrescence/outgrowth) generates a sense of the cancerous.

27. This goes far beyond Debord's *Society of the Spectacle.* 'Virtuality is different from the spectacle, which still left room for a critical consciousness and demystification. ... We are no longer spectators, but actors in the performance, and actors increasingly integrated into the course of that performance. Whereas we could face up to the unreality of the world as spectacle, we are defenceless before the extreme reality of this world, before this virtual perfection. We are, in fact, beyond all disalienation. This is the new form of terror, by comparison with which the horrors of alienation were very small beer.' *The Perfect Crime.* Translated by Chris Turner (London: Verso, 1996), p. 27.

which reality is supplanted by its models) yields to hyper-reality or integral reality (where events are definitively 'deterred'),[28] the anthropological term 'symbolic exchange' gives way to the ostensibly more accurate one of 'impossible exchange' (first used by Baudrillard in connection with the nuclear scenario of the 1970s) and to a number of variants on the notion of 'fate'.[29] The range of forms comprehended in the 'symbolic' (challenge, seduction, play, sacrifice, counter-gift) finds objective embodiment in a cluster of processes variously described as *stratégies fatales*, irreconciliation, objective irony, and later non-unification, the principle of evil or simply evil.[30]

Baudrillard sees the present work, *The Intelligence of Evil* (French title: *Le Pacte de lucidité ou l'intelligence du Mal*) as the closing text in a cycle of 'theory-fictions' that includes

28. Or to what Baudrillard sometimes simply calls reality (though this is the most paradoxical – as well as the most paroxystic – term, because it is a 'reality' with all reality 'driven out' of it (ibid., p. 4). It must be emphasized, if only because critics who should know better come to grief over this question, that the 'obvious' opposition between 'the real' and 'the virtual' was never at all pertinent for Baudrillard, who is never, as a theorist, tempted into realism ('Mais moi, je ne crois pas au réel.' *Mots de Passe*, cassette 1: de l'object au virtuel, Paris: Vidéo éditions Montparnasse, 2000). After all, reality is itself a convention, as he says in the same video, of 'framing'. And in the latest volume in the *Cool Memories* series, he writes: 'Never believed in reality: I respect it too much to believe in it.' *Cool Memories V*, 2000–2004 (Paris: Galilée, 2005), p. 9.

29. 'Actually in traditional societies exchange is absent. Symbolic exchange is the opposite of exchange. ... There is an order of exchange and an order of fate.' *Forget Foucault & Forget Baudrillard, an interview with Sylvère Lotringer* (New York: Semiotext(e), 1987), p. 84.

30. Glossing 'la stratégie fatale', Baudrillard tells Sylvère Lotringer, 'Whether you call it the revenge of the object, or the Evil Genius of matter, it is not representable. But it is a power all the same. In fact, I would go along with calling it the principle of Evil, of irreconciliation, the way the Good is the principle of reconciliation. That exists, it is inextricable, it cannot be destroyed' (ibid., p. 98).

such works as *Les stratégies fatales* (1983), *America* (1986), *The Transparency of Evil* (1990), *The Illusion of the End* (1992), *The Perfect Crime* (1995), *Impossible Exchange* (1999) and also *Télémorphose* (2001), *The Spirit of Terrorism* (2001) and *Power Inferno* (2002), not to mention the more fragmentary and aphoristic *Cool Memories* series, the fifth volume of which has just appeared. In these writings, Baudrillard has embarked on analyses that have little to do with sociology as conventionally and narrowly understood and has moved into a space of theory which he occupies with a small number of others whom he considers significant today (the list contains the names Žižek, Agamben, Sloterdijk and Virilio, but not perhaps too many more). Simply put, these works are philosophical analyses of present events and (in best Deleuzian fashion) creations and elaborations of concepts with which to 'theorize' them,[31] though the relationship between theory (perhaps the only *stratégie fatale*[32]) and events (or non-events) remains resolutely consistent with the theory itself: there are two orders – 'metaphors must remain metaphors, concepts must remain concepts' – and the relationship between them is a 'symbolic' one of *défi*, of challenge.[33]

In these 'theory-fictions', the process of 'simulation' has mutated into an even more extreme process of virtualization

---

31. In 1991, he told Anne Laurent, '*L'échange symbolique et la mort* is the last book that inspired any confidence. ... Everything I write is deemed brilliant, intelligent, but not serious. There has never been any real discussion about it. I don't claim to be tremendously serious, but there are nevertheless some philosophically serious things in my work!' 'This Beer isn't a Beer: Interview with Annie Laurent' in Mike Gane (ed.), *Baudrillard Live* (London and New York: Routledge, 1993), p. 189.

32. *Les stratégies fatales*, p. 201.

33. 'L'extase du socialisme', *A l'ombre des majorités silencieuses* (Paris: Denoël/Gonthier, 1982), pp. 103–4.

(and indeterminacy[34]), for which Baudrillard advances – at first playfully, but then with increasing force – the hypothesis that, because we are unable to bear the world of symbolic exchange (which is now transmuted into the more philosophical terminology of 'illusion'), our collective project of creating a virtual reality (in all its various forms, including such technical ventures as cloning) is to be understood as a suicidal project of termination of the human species.[35] This connects, of course, with Nietzsche's contention that humanity can only duplicate or destroy itself. Baudrillard now explicitly points up the connection also with Nietzsche's concept of the 'vital illusion'. In an interview dating from 1995, he says:

> The world of symbolic exchange was the world of illusion in the sense of the vital illusion in Nietzsche. These [primitive] societies or our earlier societies still knew how to handle this illusion. For us this radical illusion is difficult to bear. ... We replace the radical world of illusion with the relative value of simulation. ... For me the world of simulation isn't a world of alienation any longer. What is involved here is something more akin to what is perhaps a 'fateful' strategy of escaping from the world of appearance and phenomena into the world of simulation, into an artificial world that is, potentially, virtually perfect. Simulation today assumes the form of virtuality, through which we are attempting to invent a perfect, self-identical world.

34. 'Reading Baudrillard's essays since his book *Seduction* reveals a sustained but not entirely consistent attempt to think through the shift into indeterminacy' (Gane, *Jean Baudrillard: In Radical Uncertainty*, p. 96).

35. There is a 'softer' version of this thought, in which the whole of human life is presented as having become experimental, 'a limitless experimentation on human beings themselves.' See *Télémorphose* (Paris: Sens & Tonka, 2001), p. 9.

This is, of course, what Baudrillard calls the perfect crime, the 'crime, which attempts to efface its own traces'.[36] Existentially, it drops us into a world of limitless banality; morally, we have fallen into a state of indifference where we are not, in Nietzschean style, 'beyond good and evil', but where good and evil are beyond us. We are *not au-delà*, but *en-deçà*, not *jenseits*, but *diesseits*.[37]

The Intelligence of Evil or the Lucidity Pact is a book which brings political issues – or at least 'supra-political' ones, as Baudrillard puts it[38] – back to the fore. Written 'within the shadow cone of the events of 11 September', one of its central concerns is global power and the forms of resistance to it: those forms which surge up in abreaction to the excessive, prophylactic order of good, including such recognizably Baudrillardian 'objective ironies' as the globe's own 'negative reaction' to 'globalization' (below, page 29). We are back here, in dramatic form, with the system's reaction to its own perfection, with a kind of violent *transparence du mal* – a *transparence*, a 'showing-through' of evil. That phrase presents

---

36. 'Jean Baudrillard in Gespräch mit Florian Rötzer', ZKM website: *http://on1.zkm. de/zkm/ stories/storyReader$1072*. In a move that further reinforces the Nietzschean underpinnings of his position, Baudrillard here dovetails his own history of succeeding conceptions of reality into the famous passage in Nietzsche's *Götzendämmerung* on 'How the "Real World" at last Became a Myth' (see below, page 25).

37. '"Beyond Good and Evil" recalls Nietzsche and gives the impression of transcending these terms in the direction of a "higher" stage. But good and evil have already been done away with here. The global free market has no time for them. And we stand on this side [*diesseits*] of good and evil. Instead of transcendence – implosion and catastrophe.' Baudrillard interviewed by Ulrich Müller-Schöll in 'Demokratie, Menschenrechte, Markt, Liberalismus – das geht mich nichts mehr an', *Frankfurter Rundschau*, 28 November 2002.

38. Speaking on *Tout arrive*, France Culture, 11 May 2004.

a characteristic form of Baudrillardian (poetic) reversibility (and compaction). Transparency, as positive value in Enlightenment discourse and one of the great buzzwords of modern European politics, is (not without a little linguistic sleight of hand perhaps) reversed into a '*transparence* of evil', a state of affairs in which, despite all fine words and good intentions, evil repeatedly *transparaît*: i.e. shows through. *L'intelligence du mal* is a similarly polysemic, reversible title: not only does it imply an insight into 'evil' on the part of subjects, but it can signify also the intelligence of the object 'evil', the world's own greater 'understanding' of its mode of operation than is possessed by its observers. And beneath it again lies a sense of *intelligence avec le mal* in the sense in which one speaks in English of intelligence with the enemy.[39]

Speaking in 2002, Baudrillard observed that 'evil has not ceased to exist. On the contrary, it has grown, and sooner or later it explodes. Not evil as seen from a moral point of view, but something in reality itself which radically contradicts the operationalization of the world, globalization, etc.'[40] But what exactly does Baudrillard mean by evil? First, it must be said that it is to be understood not theologically as substance, but metaphysically as form. It is, as Baudrillard says elsewhere, the 'non-unification of things – good being defined as the unification of things in a totalized world' – and, as such, it

---

39. In *Cool Memories V*, Baudrillard lists a string of writers and filmmakers – Nietzsche, Céline, Kazan, Riefenstahl, Heidegger and Bellow who are condemned for *intelligence avec le mal*, for rooting their thinking in a form which is other than that of 'universal reason' and pursuing an intellectual course that has nothing to do with 'critical' intelligence, morality or political reason (pp. 132–3).
40. Müller-Schöll, 'Demokratie, Menschenrechte, Markt, Liberalismus'.

comprises for us 'all that rests on duality, on the dissociation of things, on negativity, on death'.[41]

At the level of the philosophy of history, 'evil', understood in this way, plays its part in a radically anti-Hegelian vision that draws on the dualism, the agonism of the original symbolic exchange paradigm. Whereas for Hegel and Hegelianism, despite surface conflict and contradiction, everything coheres towards unity and a higher synthesis (the *List der Vernunft* is a principle of good; the real is rational), for Baudrillard the massive, but superficial, unifying drive towards ever-greater commercial, communicational and moral-political unity in globalization, virtualization and humanitarianism is held in check by an underlying agonistic dualism: the self-moving non-unification that is 'evil', all the singular forms (not necessarily violent or terroristic) that are irreducible to this empire of the good, the process whereby power produces its own 'retroversion' and in which 'meaning destroys itself'.[42]

Against an 'integral reality' that betokens the suppression, the cancellation of all events, the elimination of any and every 'singularity', events are once again on the march. Baudrillard has in recent months added the images that came out of Abu Ghraib[43] to the 'catastrophe' of the Twin Towers (though

---

41. *Passwords.* Translated by Chris Turner (London: Verso, 2003), p. 33. Baudrillard's critique of Foucault's use of power as an explanatory principle centres on the absence of duality or reversibility within that concept. See *Forget Foucault & Forget Baudrillard*, p. 40.

42. Hence also the opposition in this text between the positive, *symbolic* notion of evil ('le mal') and the negative, *exchangeable* one of misfortune ('le malheur'), a notion that underlies all manner of compensation claims and politico-legal horse-trading.

43. See Jean Baudrillard, 'Pornography of War', *Cultural Politics* 1, 1 (2005), pp. 23–5.

catastrophe, he says disarmingly, is to be understood 'in the good sense', as 'a kind of apocalypse in the sense of a revelation'[44]) as evidence that events are again possible, that our (unreal) reality is not an absolutely terminal state. Is this *de-simulation*, as evoked in *The Illusion of the End* (1992), when the Berlin Wall had fallen and history seemed momentarily to be unfreezing? Has the possibility of the defiant, sacrificial counter-gift been reawakened?

At this point Baudrillard proposes his 'lucidity pact', and the word 'pact' is significant here. The pact is not a contract: it is not a thing of visibility – the visibility of legality and morality – but a matter of secrecy and collusion. Where analyses in terms of political realism and morality are inevitably sucked back into the media vortex to become themselves part of the unifying universe of good, can theory in some secret fashion, albeit ambiguously and dangerously, pose its 'challenge to the real':[45] can it defy, provoke and ultimately hold the world in an enigmatic, 'post-metaphysical tension'?[46]

44. 'Mais ... moi je ... donne un bon sens au mot catastrophe, je veux dire, c'est une sorte d'apocalypse au sens de révélation...'. Baudrillard speaking on *Première édition*, France Culture, 22 February 2002.

45. 'Now, theoretical concepts never offer a real alternative ... they are a *challenge* to the real. And they must remain so, on pain of turning around against you in the form of value-judgement, in the form of principles and, in particular, of that reality principle which it is their task to demolish.' 'L'extase du socialisme', *A l'ombre des majorités silencieuses*, p. 103.

46. 'Is there space for another kind of thought? An *other* thought – a paradoxical thought that would, in an inversion of the words of Marx, pose only insoluble, definitively insoluble problems? ... Is there room for a kind of thought that would instead reproblematize all the old solutions and help to hold the world in enigmatic tension? No one is certain. This may be the risk thought has to take: it must risk falling victim to its own prophecies, just as history risks getting caught in its own snare.' Baudrillard, *The Vital Illusion* (New York: Columbia University Press, 2000), p. 57.

Integral Reality

What I call Integral Reality is the perpetrating on the world of an unlimited operational project whereby everything becomes real, everything becomes visible and transparent, everything is 'liberated', everything comes to fruition and has a meaning (whereas it is in the nature of meaning that not everything has it).

Whereby there is no longer anything on which there is nothing to say.

The disappearance of God has left us facing reality and the ideal prospect of transforming this real world. And we have found ourselves confronted with the undertaking of *realizing* the world, of making it become technically, integrally real.

Now, the world, even freed from all illusion, does not lend itself at all to reality. The more we advance in this undertaking, the more ambiguous it becomes, the more it loses sight of itself. Reality has barely had time to exist and already it is disappearing...

The reality that has invented itself over recent centuries and which we have elevated into a principle is now dying out. To wish to revive it at all costs as a reference or a moral value is a mistake, since the principle is dead. What we see now, behind the eclipse of the 'objective' real, is the rise of Integral Reality, of a Virtual Reality that rests on the deregulation of the very reality principle.

We shall never get back beyond that blind spot, that unlocatable point where the real ceased to be real.

That which is real exists; that is all we can say (but existence isn't everything – it is, even, the least of things).

Let us be clear about this: when we say reality has disappeared, the point is not that it has disappeared physically, but that it has disappeared metaphysically. Reality continues to exist; it is its principle that is dead.

Now, reality without its principle is no longer the same at all. If, for many different reasons, the principle of representation, which alone gives it a meaning, falters, then the whole of the real falters. Or, rather, it exceeds its own principle and enters upon an unrestrained expansion no longer governed by any rule.

Objective reality – reality related to meaning and representation – gives way to 'Integral Reality', a reality without limits in which everything is realized and technically materialized without reference to any principle or final purpose [*destination*] whatever.

'Integral Reality' involves, then, the murder of the real, the loss of any imagination of the real.

The imaginary, which we happily associated with the real as its friendly shadow, vanishes in this same process. 'Integral Reality' has no imaginary.

Just as liberation no longer has anything to do with the play of freedom – the freedom of a subject wrestling with himself, which implies, among other things, that one remains free to be free (which is not the case in the present circumstances of unconditional liberation); just as verification puts an end to the workings of truth (for truth, if it exists, is something to be fought over, whereas verification transforms it into a *fait accompli*), so we have moved from reality as principle and as concept to the technical realization of the real and its performance.

And yet there are no proofs of this reality's existence – and there never will be – any more than there are proofs of the existence of God. It is, like God, a matter of faith.

And when you begin to believe in it, this is because it is already disappearing.

It is when one is no longer sure of the existence of God, or when one has lost the naïve faith in a self-evident reality, that it becomes absolutely necessary to believe in it.

We invested reality with the whole of our imaginary, but it is this imaginary that is vanishing, since we no longer have the energy to believe in it.

Even the will has gone out of it.

The passion for reality and the passion for truth have gone.

All that remains is a duty of reality, a duty of truth.

Henceforth we *must* believe in it. As doubt sets in everywhere, as a product of the failure of the systems of representation, reality becomes an absolute imperative; it becomes the foundation of a moral order. But neither things nor people obey a reality principle or a moral imperative.

It is the excess of reality that makes us stop believing in it.

The saturation of the world, the technical saturation of life, the excess of possibilities, of actualization of needs and desires. How are we to believe in reality once its production has become automatic?

The real is suffocated by its own accumulation. There is no way now for the dream to be an expression of a desire since its virtual accomplishment is already present.

Deprivation of dreams, deprivation of desire. And we know what mental disorder sleep deprivation induces.

Deep down, the problem is the same as with the 'accursed share': the problem of the surplus – not the lack, but the excess of reality – of which we no longer know how to rid ourselves.

There is no longer any symbolic resolution, by sacrifice, of the surplus, except in accidents or by the irruption of an anomic violence which, whatever its social or political determinations, is always a challenge to this irresistible objective constraint of a normalized world.

Effectuating, materializing, realizing, producing – it seems to be the ideal destination of everything to pass from the stage of possibility to that of reality in a movement of simultaneous progress and internal necessity.

All needs, all desires, all potentialities, tend towards this objective sanction, this litmus test. It is the same path that seems to doom appearances and illusion to vanish in the face of the truth.

Perhaps this reality is a dream; in that case, the real is part of our imaginary. And realizing everything is akin to a universal fulfilment of desire.

But today we are living through a turnabout that makes this universal fulfilment appear like a negative destiny – a catastrophic truth test. The excess of reality in all its forms, the extension of all possibilities, is becoming unbearable. Nothing is left now to the contingency of a destiny or to the non-satisfaction of desire.

Is this turn, this catastrophic inversion of effects, itself a perverse effect? Does it come under the heading of catastrophe theory? Or is it part of a universal acting-out, an inflexible logic of world-processing, the outcome of which it is impossible to predict: acceptance of a definitive reality or the collapse of that same reality, doomed to destruction by its very excess and perfection?

The eclipse of God left us up against reality.
Where will the eclipse of reality leave us?

Do we have here a negative destiny or quite simply the absence of destiny: the coming of a relentless banality, linked to the integral calculus of reality?
Destiny has not pronounced its last word.
It can be felt at the very heart of this integral realization, at the heart of this power, in that internal convulsion that follows out its logic and hastens its effects, in that maleficent reversal of the structure itself that transforms a positive destination into a murderous finality: this is where the very principle of evil lies and where the intelligence of evil must come into play.

Let us suppose two antagonistic trends:
Integral Reality: the irreversible movement towards the totalization of the world.
The Dual Form: the reversibility internal to the irreversible movement of the real.

It seems evolution (or involution) towards an integral universe is irresistible. But it seems, at the same time, that the dual form is indestructible.
There is no way for us to guess how this contradictory double movement will work itself out. We are faced with a confrontation between a dual form and total integration which cannot be resolved.

But only in appearance is there no solution, since this confrontation is constantly prey to a secret disintegration, to the dissent working away at it from the inside. It is the global violence immanent in the world-system itself which, from within, sets the purest symbolic form of the challenge against it.

There is no way to see a reconciliation here and, in all lucidity, there is nothing to tell us which force is the likely winner. Not from impartiality, since secretly we have already taken sides, but out of an awareness of the inevitability of this eternal divergence, this insuperable antagonism.

The integral drive and the dual drive: this is the Great Game.

The very idea of completion, of Integral Reality, is unbearable, but the dual form, the form that denies any final reconciliation, any definitive accomplishment, is also very difficult – and perhaps even impossible – to conceive in its radicalism.

And yet it is in this lucid vision of an endless reversion, in this denial of any objective solution, that the intelligence of evil, if it exists, is grounded.

Any questioning of reality, of its obviousness and its principle, is deemed unacceptable and condemned as negationist.[1]

The charge against you: what do you make of the reality of misery, suffering and death?

Now, it isn't about taking sides on material violence or on the violence of misfortune – it is about a line you are forbidden to cross, the line marking a taboo on reality, a taboo

---

1. The term '*négationniste*', which Baudrillard uses here in a general, neutral sense, is associated predominantly with Holocaust denial. (All footnotes in the text are my own – Tr.)

also on even the slightest attempt at interfering with a clear division between good and evil, on pain of being regarded as a scoundrel or an imposter.

The affirmation or contestation of reality, of the reality principle, is, then, a political choice, and almost a religious one, in that any infringement of this principle is sacrilegious – the very hypothesis of simulation being perceived, deep down, as diabolical (it takes up where heresy left off in the archaeology of the thinking of evil).

The reality-fundamentalists equip themselves with a form of magical thinking that confuses message and messenger: if you speak of the simulacrum, then you are a simulator; if you speak of the virtuality of war, then you are in league with it and have no regard for the hundreds of thousands of dead.

Any analysis other than the moral is condemned as deluded or irresponsible.

Now, if reality is a question of belief and all the signs that attested to it have lost their credibility, if the real has fallen into fundamental discredit and its principle is everywhere reeling, it is not we, the messengers of the simulacrum, who have plunged things into this discredit, it is the system itself that has fomented this uncertainty that affects everything today – even the sense of existence.

What looms on the horizon with the advent of globalization is the constitution of an integral power, of an Integral Reality of power and an equally integral and automatic disintegration and failure of that power.

A dramatic form of reversibility.

A sort of turnabout, revenge and devastating irony, a kind of negative reaction on the part of the world itself against globalization.

All the forces denied and expelled by this very process, which thereby become the forces of evil, rebel. Power itself fights against becoming total: it passes the buck; it disinvests itself; in the end it works secretly against itself.

To speak evil is to describe the growing hegemony of the powers of good and, at the same time, their inner faltering, their suicidal crumbling, their reversion, their outgrowth and separation into parallel universes once the dividing line of the Universal has been crossed.

On the Fringes of the Real

We have abolished the real world: what world is left? the apparent world perhaps?... But no! with the real world we have also abolished the apparent world!

Friedrich Nietzsche

If we are not to believe that truth remains truth when we lift its veil, then truth has no naked existence.

And if we are not to believe that the real remains the real when we have dispelled its illusion, then the real has no objective reality.

What becomes of the world when freed from truth and appearances? It becomes the real universe, the universe of Integral Reality. Neither truth nor appearance, but Integral Reality.

If, in the past, the world reached towards transcendence, and if, in the process, it fell into other hinterworlds, it has today fallen into reality.

If there was in the past an upward transcendence, there is today a downward one. This is, in a sense, the second Fall of Man Heidegger speaks of: the fall into banality, but this time without any possible redemption.

Once the real world has been lost, at the same time as the world of appearances, says Nietzsche, the universe becomes a universe of fact, a positive universe, a universe 'as is', which no longer even has any need to be true. As factual as a ready-made.

Duchamp's *Fountain* is the emblem of our modern hyper-reality, the product of a violent counter-transference of all poetic illusion on to pure reality, the object 'transferred' on to itself, short-circuiting any possible metaphor.

The world has acquired such a degree of reality that it is bearable only by a perpetual denial, with 'This is not a world' – reminiscent of Magritte's 'This is not a pipe' – operating as the surrealist denial of self-evidence itself, this dual movement of the absolute, definitive obviousness of the world and the equally radical denial of that obviousness dominating the trajectory of modern art.

And not just the trajectory of art, but of all our deep perceptions, of our entire mental apprehension of the world.

It is no longer a matter here of philosophical morality of the sort that says 'the world isn't what it ought to be' or 'the world isn't what it was'.

No, the world is as it is.

Once all transcendence is conjured away, things are no longer anything but what they are and, such as they are, they are unbearable. All illusion is gone from them and they have become immediately and totally real, with no shadow and no commentary.

And, at the same time, this insurmountable reality no longer exists. It has no grounds for existence any more, since it is no longer exchangeable for anything and has no opposite term.

'Does reality exist? Are we in a real world?' – this is the leitmotiv of our entire present culture. But it merely expresses the fact that we can no longer bear this world, which is so prey to reality, except by way of a radical denial. And this is logical: since the world can no longer be justified in another world, it has to be justified here and now in this one by lending itself force of reality, by purging itself of any illusion. But at the same time, by the very effect of this counter-transference, the denial of the real as such grows.

Reality, having lost its natural predators, is growing like some proliferating species. A little bit like algae or even like the human race in general.

The Real is growing like the desert. 'Welcome to the Desert of the Real'.

Illusion, dreams, passion, madness and drugs, but also artifice and simulacrum – these were reality's natural predators. They have all lost energy, as though struck down by some dark, incurable malady. We have, then, to find an artificial equivalent for them, since, if we do not, reality, once it has attained its critical mass, will end up destroying itself spontaneously, will implode of its own accord – which it is, in fact, currently doing, giving way to the Virtual in all its forms.

It is in the Virtual that we have the ultimate predator and plunderer of reality, secreted by reality itself as a kind of self-destructive viral agent.

Reality has fallen prey to Virtual Reality, the final consequence of the process begun with the abstraction of objective reality – a process that ends in Integral Reality.

What we have in virtuality is no longer a hinterworld: the substitution of the world is total; this is the identical doubling of the world, its perfect mirroring, and the matter is settled by the pure and simple annihilation of symbolic substance. Even objective reality becomes a useless function, a kind of waste that is ever more difficult to exchange and circulate.

We have moved, then, from objective reality to a later stage, a kind of ultra-reality that puts an end to both reality and illusion.

Integral Reality is also to be found in integral music: the sort you find in quadraphonic spaces or can 'compose' on a computer. The music in which sounds have been clarified and expurgated and which, shorn of all noise and static, is, so to speak, restored to its technical perfection. The sounds of such music are no longer the play of a form, but the actualization of a programme. It is a music reduced to a pure wavelength, the final reception of which, the tangible effect on the listener, is exactly programmed too, as in a closed circuit. It is, in a sense, a virtual music, flawless and without imagination, merging into its own model, and even the enjoyment of it is virtual enjoyment. Is this still music? The question must be open to doubt, since they have actually come up with the idea of reintroducing noise into it to make it more 'musical'.

The computer-generated image is like this too, a digital image which is entirely fabricated, has no real referent and from which, by contrast with analogue images, the negative itself has disappeared – not just the film negative, but the negative moment that lies at the heart of the image, that absence that causes the image to resonate. The technical fine-tuning here is perfect. There is no room for fuzziness, tremor or chance. Is this still an image?

Going further on these lines, we come to the very principle of Integral Man, reworked by genetics with an eye to perfection. With every accidental feature excised, all physiological or emotional pathology removed. Because what genetic manipulation is aiming at is not an original formula of the human, but the most conformable, most efficient formula ('serial morphing').

We get a foretaste of this in Stephen Spielberg's *Minority Report*, in which the crime is prevented – and the sentence handed down – before it has even taken place and without our ever knowing whether it would have happened. Nipped in the bud in its very imagining, in accordance with the universal precautionary principle.

Yet the film is anachronistic, as it still involves policing, whereas future crime prevention will be genetic, intragenic: the 'criminal gene' will be surgically removed at birth – or even before – by a kind of prophylactic sterilization (which will very quickly have to become quite widespread since, from the police standpoint, which is that of power, we are all potential criminals).

This manipulation tells us precisely what the future human being will be. He will be a corrected, rectified human. He will be from the outset what he should have been ideally. He will never, therefore, become what he is. He won't even be alienated any longer, since he will be modified pre-existentially, for better or for worse.

There isn't even any danger of his encountering his own otherness, since he will, from the outset, have been devoured by his own model.

All this is based on a universal process of eradication of evil.

Evil, which was once a metaphysical or moral principle, is today pursued materially right down into the genes (and also in the 'Axis of Evil'). It has become an objective reality and hence objectively eliminable. We are going to be able to excise it at the root, and with it, increasingly, all dreams, utopias, illusions and fantasies – all these things being, by the same general process, wrested from the possible to be put back into the real.

This absolute reality is also that of money when it passes from the relative abstraction of exchange-value to the purely speculative stage of the virtual economy. Marx in his day argued that the movement of exchange-value was more real than mere use-value, but, in our situation, where capital flows are unrelated to commodity exchange, money becomes an even stranger hyperreality: it becomes absolute money; it attains the Integral Reality of calculus. Being no longer the equivalent of anything, it becomes the object of a universal passion. The hieroglyph of the commodity has become the integral fetishism of money.

Last but not least comes that surgical operation on language whereby, in its digital version, its entire symbolic dimension is eliminated, that is to say, whereby everything that makes it much more than merely what it signifies is removed... All there is in it of absence and emptiness, but also of literalness, is eliminated, just like the negative in the computer-generated image – all that stands opposed to an exclusive clarification. Such is the Integral Reality of language: it now signifies only what it signifies.

Time itself, lived time, no longer has time to take place. The historical time of events, the psychological time of affects and passion, the subjective time of judgement and will, are all simultaneously called into question by virtual time, which is called, no doubt derisively, 'real time'.[2]

It is, in fact, no accident if space-time is called 'real'. *Temps réel, Echtzeit*: this is 'authentic' time, non-deferred time, the time of an instantaneous presence that is no longer even the present moment in relation to a past or a future, but a point of convergence, and at the same time of cancellation, of all the other dimensions. An Integral Reality of time that is now concerned with nothing but its own operation: time-processing (like 'word-processing', 'war-processing', etc.).

2. This phrase is in English in the original.

With this notion of 'real time', all dimensions have contracted to a single focal point, to a fractal form of time. The differential of time having disappeared, it is the integral function that wins out: the immediate total presence of a thing to itself, which signifies that reality is henceforth the privilege of that which is identical with itself. All that is absent from itself, all that differs from itself, is not truly real.

This whole business is, of course, pure fantasy.

Nothing and no one is absolutely present to itself, herself or himself (or, *a fortiori*, to others). So nothing and no one is truly real and real time does not exist.

We do not even perceive the sun in real time, since the speed of light is relative. And so it is with everything.

In this sense, reality is inconceivable. Integral Reality is a utopia. And yet this is what, by a gigantic artifice, is being imposed upon us.

Behind the immateriality of the technologies of virtual reality, of the digital and the screen, there lies a hidden injunction, an imperative McLuhan had already identified in the TV and media image: that of a heightened participation, of an interactive investment that may reach dizzying proportions, that may go so far as the 'ecstatic' involvement we see everywhere in the cyberworld.

Immersion, immanence and immediacy – these are the characteristics of the Virtual.

There is no gaze any longer, no scene, no imaginary, no illusion even, no longer any exteriority or spectacle: the operational fetish has absorbed all exteriority, reclaimed all interiority, absorbed time itself in the operation of real time.

In this way we come closer to a world that is integrally realized, that is effectuated and identified as such, but not closer to *the world as it is*, which is something quite different.

For the world-as-it-is is of the order of appearances, if not indeed of integral illusion, since there is no possible representation of it.

Two hypotheses on this fatal strategy of the trans-digitization of the world into pure information, of cloning of the real by Virtual Reality, of substitution of a technical, artificial universe for the 'natural' world.

The first is the hypothesis of the radical illusoriness of the world – that is to say, of the impossibility of exchanging the world for any ultimate truth or purpose.

Such as it is, the world is without causal explanation or possible representation (any mirror whatever would still be part of the world).

Now, that for which there is neither a meaning nor a definitive reason is an illusion.

The world therefore has all the characteristics of a thoroughgoing illusion.

For us, however, whatever its metaphysical beauty, this illusion is unbearable. Hence the need to produce all the possible forms of a simulacrum of meaning, of transcendence – things which all mask this original illusoriness and protect us from it.

Thus the simulacrum is not that which hides the truth, but that which hides the absence of truth.

It is in this perspective that the invention of reality has its place.

In the shadow of reality, of this causal and rational simulation model, the exchange of the world becomes possible, since it is defined by objective laws.

Second hypothesis: the world is given to us. Now, in accordance with the symbolic rule, when something is given to us, we must be able to give it back.

In the past, we could give thanks in one way or another to God or some other agency; we could respond to the gift with a sacrifice.

But now that all transcendence has disappeared we no longer have anyone to whom to give thanks. And if we can give nothing in exchange for this world, it is unacceptable.

It is for this reason that we find ourselves having to liquidate the natural world and substitute an artificial one for it – a world built from scratch and for which we will be accountable to no one.

Hence the gigantic undertaking of eliminating the natural world in all its forms. All that is natural will be denied in the more or less long term by virtue of this enforced substitution. The Virtual appears here as the final solution to the impossible exchange of the world.

But in itself this does not settle the matter, as we shall never escape this new debt, contracted in this instance with ourselves. How are we to absolve ourselves of this technical world and this artificial omnipotence?

Here again, for want of being able to exchange this world (for what?), we need to destroy or deny it. Which explains, at the same time as we progress in building up this artificial universe, the immense negative counter-transference against this Integral Reality we have forged for ourselves.

A deep-seated denial that is present everywhere today. So that we do not know which will win out in the end, this irresistible technical undertaking or the violent reaction against it.

At all events, the undertaking is never complete.

We are never done with making good the void of truth.

Hence the flight forward into ever more simulacra.

Hence the invention of an increasingly artificial reality such that there is no longer anything standing over against it or any ideal alternative to it, no longer any mirror or negative.

With the very latest Virtual Reality we are entering a final phase of this entreprise of simulation, which ends this time in an artificial technical production of the world from which all trace of illusion has disappeared.

A world so real, hyperreal, operational and programmed that it no longer has any need to be true. Or rather it is true, absolutely true, in the sense that nothing any longer stands opposed to it.

We have here the absurdity of a total truth from which falsehood is lacking – that of absolute good from which evil is lacking, of the positive from which the negative is lacking.

If the invention of reality is the substitute for the absence of truth, then, when the self-evidence of this 'real' world becomes generally problematic, does this not mean that we are closer to the absence of truth – that is to say, to the world as it is?

We are certainly further and further removed from the solution, but nearer and nearer to the problem.

For the world is not real. It became real, but it is in the process of ceasing to be so. But it is not virtual either – though it is on the way to becoming so.

It is against this world become entirely operational, objective and without alternative that the denial of reality, the disavowal of reality, develops.

If the world is to be taken *en bloc*, then it is at that point we reject it *en bloc*. There is no other solution. This is a rejection similar to the biological rejection of a foreign body.

It is by a kind of instinct, a kind of vital reaction, that we rebel against this immersion in a completed world, in the 'Kingdom of Heaven', in which real life is sacrificed to the hyperrealization of all its possibilities, to its optimum performance, in much the way the species is sacrificed today to its genetic perfection.

Our negative abreaction is the product of our hypersensitivity to the ideal conditions of life provided for us.

This perfect reality, to which we sacrifice all illusion the way that all hope is left behind on the threshold of Hell, is quite obviously a phantom reality.

We are pained by it precisely as we would be by a phantom limb:

Yet, as Ahab says in *Moby Dick*: 'And if I still feel the smart of my crushed leg, though it be now so long dissolved; then, why mayst not thou, carpenter, feel the fiery pains of hell for ever, and without a body?'[3]

There is nothing metaphorical about this sacrifice. It is, rather, of the order of a surgical operation, which, moreover, becomes something of a source of pleasure for itself: 'Humankind, which once in Homer, was an object of contemplation for the Olympian gods, has now become one for itself. Its self-alienation has reached the point where it can experience its own annihilation as a supreme aesthetic pleasure.'[4]

One of the possibilities is, in fact, self-destruction – an exceptional one in that it is a defiance of all the others.

---

3. Herman Melville, *Moby Dick*, translated by Edmund Jephcott and Harry Zohn, (Harmondsworth: Penguin, 2003), pp. 513–14.
4. Walter Benjamin, 'The Work of Art in the Age of its Reproducibility', in *Selected Writings*, vol. III (Cambridge, MA/London: Belknap Press of Harvard University Press, 2002), p. 122.

A twofold illusion: that of an objective reality of the world, that of a subjective reality of the subject – which are refracted in the same mirror and merged in the same founding movement of our metaphysics.

The world, for its part, isn't objective at all and may be said, rather, to take the form of a 'strange attractor'.

But because the seduction of the world and of appearances is dangerous, we prefer to exchange it for its operational simulacrum, its artificial truth and its *automatic writing*. However, that very protection is perilous since everything we use to defend ourselves against this vital illusion, our entire defence strategy, functions as a veritable character armour and itself becomes unbearable.

In the end, it is the strangeness of the world that is fundamental and it is that strangeness which resists the status of objective reality.

Similarly, it is our strangeness to ourselves that is fundamental and resists the status of subject.

It is not a matter of resisting alienation, but of resisting the very status of subject.

In all these forms of disavowal, nay-saying and denial, what is at work is not a dialectic of negativity or the 'work of the negative'. It is no longer a question of a thought critical of reality, but of a subversion of reality in its principle, in its very self-evidence. The greater the positivity, the more violent is the – possibly silent – denial. We are all dissidents of reality today, clandestine dissidents most of the time.

If thought cannot be exchanged for reality, then the immediate denial of reality becomes the only reality-based thinking. But this denial does not lead to hope, as Adorno would have it: 'Hope, as it emerges from reality by struggling against it to deny it, is the only manifestation of lucidity.' Whether for good or for ill, this is not true.

Hope, if we were still to have it, would be hope for intelligence of – for insight into – good. Now, what we have left is intelligence of evil, that is to say, intelligence not of a critical reality, but of a reality that has become unreal by dint of positivity, that has become speculative by dint of simulation.

Because it is there to counter a void, the whole enterprise of simulation and information, this aggravation of the real and of knowledge of the real, merely gives rise to an evergreater uncertainty. Its very profusion and relentlessness simply spreads panic.

And that uncertainty is irredeemable, as it is made up of all the possible solutions.

Are we irremediably the captives of this transference of the real into a total positivity and of the equally massive countertransference that tends towards its pure and simple denial?

Whereas everything is driving us towards this totalization of the real, *we must, rather, wrest the world from its reality principle.* For it is this confusion that conceals from us the world as it is, that is to say, at bottom, the world as singularity.

Italo Svevo: 'The search for causes is an immense misunderstanding, a deep-rooted superstition that prevents things, events from occurring as they are.'

The real is of the order of generality; the world is of the order of singularity. That is to say, of an absolute difference, a radical difference, something more different than difference – at the farthest possible remove from this confusion of the world with its double.

Something definitively resists us, something other than truth or reality.

Something resists all our efforts to confine the world to a sequence of causes and effects.

There is an elsewhere of reality (most cultures do not even have the concept). Something from before the so-called 'real' world, something irreducible, linked to primal illusion and to the impossibility of giving the world as it is any kind of ultimate meaning whatever.

Wishing, knowing and feeling are inextricably intertwined. But there is perhaps a way of moving through the world other than by following the thread of the real.

Robert Musil

On the World in Its Profound Illusoriness

The invention of Reality, unknown to other cultures, is the work of modern western Reason, the turn to the Universal. The turn to an objective world, shorn of all hinterworlds.

Concretizing, verifying, objectivizing, demonstrating: 'objectivity' is this capture of the real that forces the world to face us, expurgating it of any secret complicity, of any illusion.

We always imagine the Real as something face on. We think of ourselves always as facing the Real. Well, there is no face to-face. There is no objectivity. Nor any subjectivity either: a twofold illusion.

Since consciousness is an integral part of the world and the world is an integral part of consciousness, I think it and it thinks me.

One need only reflect that even if objects exist outside of us, we can know absolutely nothing of their objective reality. For things are given to us only through our representation. To believe that these representations and sensations are determined by external objects is a further representation.

'The question whether things really exist outside of us and as we see them is absolutely meaningless. ... The question is almost as absurd as wondering whether blue is really blue, objectively blue' (Georg Christoph Lichtenberg).[5]

5. Where I have been able to trace the fragments from Lichtenberg's work, I have referred to them using the classification system established in the six-volume edition published by W. Promies (Munich: Hanser, 1968–92).

This is something we definitively cannot judge. We can only represent an objective reality to ourselves, without ever pre-judging its objectivity. If such objects do exist outside of us, we can know absolutely nothing of them, and there is nothing to be said about them...

The task of philosophy is to unmask this illusion of objective reality – a trap that is, in a sense, laid for us by nature.

'Nothing so clearly reveals the superior mind of man than his having been able to unmask nature at the precise point where it was attempting to deceive him' (Lichtenberg).[6]

But this is where philosophy stops – at the definitive acknowledgement of the illusoriness of the world. That is to say, at that point, that object, that something, that nothing, of which there is nothing more to be said.

The philosophical idea is, then, simple and radical: it is the idea of a fundamental illusoriness, of the non-reality of the 'objective' world.

This representation, this superstition of an objective reality held out to us by the mirror of the commonplace imagination, is itself a part of the general illusion of the world, of which we are a part at the same time as we are its mirror.

There is not just the illusion of a real world, there is also that of a real subject of representation – and the two illusions, the objective and the subjective, are correlative.

This is where the mystery lies.

For the world does not exist in order for us to know it,

It is not in any way predestined for knowledge. However, knowledge is itself part of the world, though precisely part *of the world in its profound illusoriness, which consists in having no necessary relation to knowledge.*

6. Fragment H 151.

This is the miracle: that a fragment of the world, human consciousness, arrogates to itself the privilege of being its mirror. But this will never produce an objective truth, since the mirror is part of the object it reflects.

The current microsciences have taken cognizance of this definitive illusion, which is not the illusion of an objective non-truth (that would still have the prestige of reality for itself), but of the entangling of two illusions, objective and subjective, of their inextricable complicity, which properly prevents any metaphysical reflection of the world by thought.

This is the trap nature sets for us.

The dilemma, which is that of an impossible equivalence, an impossible correlation between the object and its 'objective' representation, arises from this circularity, this reversibility of a process that can no longer then be called representation.

And it is an irresolvable one because reversibility is there from the outset. *It* is the fundamental rule.

'It is impossible for a being to undergo the effect of some other without that effect being mutual. ... Every effect modifies the object that is its cause. There is no dissociation of the subject and the object – nor any original identity – there is only an inextricable reciprocity' (Lichtenberg).

Reversibility of the self and the world:

'Everything happens in the world of the self. This self, within which everything unfolds, resembles in this regard the cosmos of physics, to which the self also belongs by which that cosmos appeared mentally in our representation. ... So the circle is complete' (Lichtenberg).

A circle which is that of an infinite embedding, in which the subject cannot lay claim to a determinate position anywhere, and in which the object is not localizable as such either.

What we have here might be said to be not so much a form of alienation as a perpetual becoming-object of the subject, a perpetual becoming-subject of the object. Once again, the world does not exist in order for us to know it or, more exactly, knowledge itself is part of the illusion of the world – and this is not an objection, far from it: it is here, in this insoluble affinity, that the secret of thought lies.

This is the very principle of the world that thinks us.

The question of whether there is an objective reality does not even arise: the intelligence of the world is the intelligence of the world that thinks us.

It is the created object which thinks us, and which sometimes thinks better than we do, and quicker than we do: which thinks us before we have thought it.

This paradoxical essence of man, who, though an integral part of nature, still tries to see how it could be for him beyond that state of belonging, puts us in mind of what Nietzsche says in his metaphor of the mirror:

'When we try to examine the mirror in itself we discover in the end nothing but things upon it. If we want to grasp the things we finally get hold of nothing but the mirror. – This, in the most general terms, is the history of knowledge.'[7]

This speculative abyss deepens yet again if we move from the mirror to the total screen of Virtual Reality.

This time it is not nature that lays the trap of objective reality for us, but the digital universe which sets us the trap of a hyperobjectivity, of an integral calculus in which the very play of the mirror and its objects is abolished – the last

---

7. *Daybreak: Thoughts on the Prejudices of Morality.* Translated by R. J. Hollingdale with an introduction by Michael Tanner (Cambridge: Cambridge Univesity Press, 1982), p. 141.

avatar of philosophical idealism. At the same time, it puts an irrevocable end to that hyperobjectivity, since the principle of representation itself disappears beneath the calculation and digital generation of operations. As a result, all that remains is to occupy that non-place, that pre-eminent empty space of representation that is the screen.

All this follows a kind of dizzying whirl, as though this growing abstraction, this rise of an integral hyperreality, were itself a response to a hypersensitivity to certain final conditions.
But what final conditions?

Reality will have been only a fleeting solution then.
Indeed, it merely succeeded others, such as the religious illusion in all its forms. This truth, this rationality, this object-ive reality – which we took in exchange for religious values, imagining that we had moved definitively beyond them – is only the disenchanted heir to those same religious values. It does not seem ever genuinely to have gained the upper hand, as it happens, nor does it appear that the transcendent solution is entirely past and gone or that God is dead, even though we now deal only with his metastases.
Perhaps that solution was merely eclipsed and it is emerging from its eclipse in reaction to this very intensification of reality, to the weight of an ever more real, ever more secular world in which there is no possibility of redemption.
Reality too is a hinterworld and a substitutive illusion, and in fact we live in this 'real' world as in a hinterworld. It is merely that we have succeeded in negotiating it in a way that does without heaven and hell (though not without debt and guilt, for which we are now answerable to ourselves).
Have we gained or lost on the deal? There is no answer.
We have exchanged one illusion for another, and it turns out that the material, objective illusion, the illusion of reality,

is as fragile as the illusion of God and no longer protects us, once the euphoria of science and the Enlightenment is past, from the fundamental illusion of the world and its absence of truth.

In fact, this secular, desacralized reality has slowly become a useless function, the fiction of which we are desperately attempting to rescue (as once we attempted to rescue the existence of God), but which, deep down, we do not know how to rid ourselves of.

This is where the last phase of the enterprise comes in.

Given reality's powerlessness to bridge the gap that separates us from the world and the insoluble enigma it presents for us, we have had to move to a further stage – that of the Virtual, Virtual Reality, the highest stage of simulation, the stage of a final solution by the volatilization of the world's substance into an immaterial realm and a set of strategic calculations.

God, who once was present, but also absent, from all things, now circulates in the arterial network of computers.

The play of transcendence is over, the paradoxical play of presence and absence. What remains is an integral form of reality, of which we are all operators.

What was still merely a relative idealism gives way to an absolute idealism, that of the new computer technologies, in which the fragile balance of subject and object is swept away and total abstraction takes its place.

This is the very end of the illusion of the object and hence of philosophy which defined itself, after all, by this point beyond which it had nothing more to say.

Henceforth the question no longer arises, since there isn't even any subject to pose it now. The very position of the subject is eclipsed in this integral functioning.

We are, in fact, in pure pataphysics, pataphysics being, on the one hand, the science of imaginary solutions and, on the other, the only known attempt to move to Integral Metaphysics, the metaphysics in which the phenomenal world is treated definitively as an illusion.

Now, this is precisely what we are up against with the XXX phase of reality that we have arrived at...

Objective reality corresponded to an horizon for metaphysics.

Integral Reality corresponds to the pataphysical sphere.

There is no more marvellous embodiment of Integral Reality than Ubu. Ubu is the very symbol of this plethoric reality and, at the same time, the only response to this Integral Reality, the only solution that is truly imaginary in its fierce irony, its grotesque fullness. The great spiral belly of Pa Ubu is the profile of our world and its umbilical entombment.

We are not yet done with pataphysics, that science which 'symbolically attributes to their lineaments the properties of objects, described in their potentiality' (Alfred Jarry).[8]

But the die is not cast, since, though the real is growing as a result of a breaking of the symbolic pact between beings and things, that break gives rise, in its turn, to a tenacious resistance, the rejection of an objective world, a separate world. Deep down, no one desires this objective face-to-face relation, even in the privileged role of subject.

What binds us to the real is a contract of reality. That is to say, a formal awareness of the rights and duties attaching to reality. But what we long for is a complicity and dual relation with beings and things – a pact, not a contract. Hence the

---

8. Alfred Jarry, *Exploits and Opinions of Doctor Faustroll, 'Pataphysician*, Book II, Chapter 8 (1907). My translation.

temptation to condemn this contract – along with the social contract that ensues from it.

Against the moral contract that binds us to reality we must set a pact of intelligence and lucidity.

Having said this, on the verge of this dramatic changeover, we may still ask the question:

Is the end of history still a historical fact?

Is the disappearance of reality still a real fact?

No, it is an accomplished fact and, in the face of accomplished facts, it is not objectivity, but defiance that is in order. We must defy reality as we must defy any accomplished fact.

The Easiest Solutions

The hypothesis of objective reality exerts such a hold on our minds only because it is by far the easiest solution.

Lichtenberg: 'That a false hypothesis is sometimes preferable to an exact one is proven in the doctrine of human freedom. Man is, without a doubt, unfree. But it takes profound philosophical study for a man not to be led astray by such an insight. Barely one in a thousand has the necessary time and patience for such study, and of these hundreds, barely one has the necessary intelligence. This is why freedom is the most convenient conception and will, in the future, remain the most common, so much do appearances favour it.'[9]

The exact hypothesis is that man is born unfree, that the world is born untrue, non-objective, non-rational. But this radical hypothesis is definitively beyond proof, unverifiable and, in a sense, unbearable. Hence the success of the opposite hypothesis, of the easiest hypothesis.

Subjective illusion: that of freedom.

Objective illusion: that of reality.

Just as belief in freedom is merely the illusion of being the cause of one's own acts, so the belief in objective reality is the illusion of finding an original cause for phenomena and hence of inserting the world into the order of truth and reason.

9. Fragment J 278.

Despairing of confronting otherness, seduction, the dual relation and destiny, we invent the easiest solution: freedom. First, the ideal concept of a subject wrestling with his own freedom. Then, *de facto* liberation, unconditional liberation – the highest stage of freedom.

We pass from the right to freedom to the categorical imperative of liberation.

But to this stage, too, there is the same violent abreaction: we rid ourselves of freedom in every way possible, even going so far as to invent new servitudes.

Despairing of confronting uncertainty and radical illusion, we invent the easiest solution: reality.

First, objective reality, then Integral Reality – the highest stage of reality.

To this highest stage there corresponds the equally radical disavowal of that same reality. Violent abreaction to Integral Reality – negative counter-transference.

Despairing of an aim, salvation or an ideal, we invent for ourselves the easiest solution: happiness.

Here again we begin with utopia – the ideal of happiness – and end in achieved happiness, the highest stage of happiness. The same abreaction to integral happiness as to integral reality or freedom: these are all unbearable.

In the end, it is the opposite form of misfortune, the victim ideology, that triumphs.

Being incapable of accepting thought (the idea that the world thinks us, the intelligence of evil), we invent the easiest solution, the technical solution: Artificial Intelligence.

The highest stage of intelligence: integral knowledge.

This time the rejection will arise perhaps from a resistance on the part of things themselves to their digital transparency or from a failure of the system in the form of a major accident.

Against all the sovereign hypotheses are ranged the easiest solutions.
And all the easiest solutions lead to catastrophe.

Against the hypothesis of uncertainty: the illusion of truth and reality.
Against the hypothesis of destiny: the illusion of freedom.
Against the hypothesis of evil [*Mal*]: the illusion of misfortune [*malheur*].
Against the hypothesis of thought, the illusion of Artificial Intelligence.
Against the hypothesis of the event: the illusion of information.
Against the hypothesis of becoming: the illusion of change.

Every easy solution, pushed to its extreme – Integral Reality, integral freedom, integral happiness, integral information (the highest stage of intelligence, the highest stage of reality, the highest stage of freedom, the highest stage of happiness) – finds a response in a violent abreaction: disavowal of reality, disavowal of freedom, disavowal of happiness, viruses and dysfunctions, spectrality of real time, mental resistance; all the forms of secret repulsion in respect of this ideal normalization of existence.
Which proves that there still exists everywhere, in each of us, resisting the universal beatification, an intelligence of evil.

Do You Want to be Free?

Freedom? A dream!

Everyone aspires to it, or at least gives the impression of aspiring fervently to it.

If it is an illusion, it has become a vital illusion.

In morality, mores and mentalities, this movement, which seems to well up from the depths of history, is towards irrevocable emancipation.

And if some aspects may seem excessive or contradictory, we still experience the dizzying thrill of this emancipation.

Better: the whole of our system turns this liberation into a duty, a moral obligation – to the point where it is difficult to distinguish this liberation compulsion from a 'natural' aspiration towards, a 'natural' demand for, freedom.

Now, it is clear that, where all forms of servitude are concerned, everyone wants to throw them off; where all forms of constraint are concerned – physical constraints or constraints of law – everyone wishes to be free of them. This is such a vital reaction that there is barely, in the end, any need of an idea of freedom to express it.

Things become problematic when the prospect arises for the subject of being answerable solely for him/herself in an undifferentiated universe. For this symbolic disobligation is accompanied by a general deregulation. And it is in this universe of free electrons – free to become anything whatever in a system of generalized exchange – that we see growing, simultaneously, a contrary impulse, a resistance to this availability of everyone and everything that is every bit as deep as the desire for freedom. A passion for rules of whatever kind that is equal to the passion for deregulation.

In the anthropological depths of the species, the demand for rules is as fundamental as the demand to be free of them.

No one can say which is the more basic.

What we can see, after a long period of ascendancy for the process of liberation, is the resurrection of all those movements that are more and more steadfastly resistant to boundless emancipation and total immunity.

A desire for rules that has nothing to do with submission to the law. It might even be said to run directly counter to it, since, whereas the law is abstract and universal, the rule, for its part, is a two-way obligation. And it is neither of the order of law, nor of duty, nor of moral and psychological law.

Regarded everywhere as an absolute advance of the human race, and with the seal set on it by human rights, liberation starts out from the idea of a natural predestination to be free: being 'liberated' absolves the human being of an original evil, restores a happy purpose and a natural vocation to him. It is our salvation, the true baptismal sacrament of modern, democratic man.

Now, this is a utopia.

This impulse to resolve the ambivalence of good and evil and jump over one's shadow into absolute positivity is a utopia.

The ambivalence is definitive, and the things liberated are liberated in total ambivalence.

You cannot liberate good without liberating evil. Sometimes evil even quicker than good, as part of the same movement.

At any rate, what we have here is a deregulation of both.

Liberation opens up a limitless growth and acceleration.

It is once this critical threshold has been crossed (this phase transition, much as in the physical world) that things begin to float – time, money, sex, production – in a vertiginous raising of the stakes, such as we are experiencing today, which brings an uncontrollable eruption of all autonomies, all differences, in a movement that is at once uncertain, fluctuating and exponential.

At this point freedom is already far behind, overtaken and outdistanced by liberation.

What is forming before us is a freedom of circulation of each autonomized human particle under the banner of total information and integration. Each one realizing itself fully in the technical extension of all its possibilities: all stakeholders and partners in a general interaction. Only the God of the Market will recognize his own, and the 'Invisible Hand' is now the weightless ascendancy of software and networks in the name of Universal Free Exchange – the highest stage of deregulation.

A logical, fateful consquence of a dynamic that seems to be at work from the origin of historical societies – the dynamic of a progressive, universal deregulation of all human relations.

From feudalism to capital and beyond, what we see is, above all, an immense advance in the freedom of exchange, in the free circulation of goods, flows, persons and capital.

The movement is irreversible, not in terms of human progress but in terms of the market, of the progressive advance of an inescapable globalization.

This is the last stage liberalism passes through in its unremitting advance towards generalized exchange, a process of which capital, with its conflicts, contradictions, violent history – simply with its 'history' – is ultimately just the prehistory.

However, we see resistance to this second 'revolution' springing up on all sides – forms of resistance even more intense than those aroused by the advent of the Enlightenment: all these movements of re-involution (the opposite of revolution), whether religious, sectarian or corporatist, new fundamentalisms or new feudalisms, which simply seem to be trying to rid themselves everywhere of this unconditional freedom and find new forms of oversight, protection and vassalage, to counter an unbearable disaffiliation with an archaic fidelity.

To counter deregulation with a new set of rules.

It may even be that the only refuge from the global, from a total exposure to the laws of the market, will once again be the condition of wage-earner, the 'social' with its institutional protection.

In other words, a defence of the good old 'alienated' condition, though protected by its very alienation, as it were, from overexposure to the laws of flows and networks alone. With this 'voluntary' alienation possibly extending as far as an even more archaic regression to any kind of protective transcendence that offers preservation from this scattering about the networks, this dispersion and dissemination into the void.

Only now do we realize we shall never be done with this paradox of freedom. For this irreversible movement of emancipation can be seen either as progress on the part of the species (it is, at any rate, this emancipation that ensures the superiority of the human species over all others) or, in a quite opposite way, as an anthropological catastrophe, an unbinding, a dizzying deregulation, whose ultimate goal we cannot grasp but which seems to be developing towards an unforeseeable extreme that may either be the highest stage of universal intelligence or of total entropy.

We pass the buck on freedom in every possible way.

In a continual transference, we devolve our own desires, our own lives, our own wills, to any other agency whatever.

If the people puts itself in the hands of the political class, it does so more to be rid of power than out of any desire for representation. We may interpret this as a sign of passivity and irresponsibility, but why not venture a subtler hypothesis: namely, that this passing of the buck proceeds from an unwittingly lucid intuition of an absence of desire and will of their own – in short, a secret awareness of the illusoriness of freedom?

'Voluntary servitude'?

The notion is doubly illusory, since it encapsulates in itself the double mystification of the two concepts of freedom and will. And the idea of a will, understood as autonomous determination of the individual being, is no less false when it turns round against freedom.

The illusion does not necessarily lie where one thinks it does, and if a few only (Lichtenberg) are able to know that they are 'unfree' and to accept that destiny, the great bulk of the others ultimately have fewer illusions about their free will than those who created the concept.

This does not stop 'voluntary servitude' having its rules and strategies

It is by the absence of a desire of one's own that the other's will to dominate is thwarted: these are the ruses of seduction.

It is by transferring the responsibility of power on to the other that a form of equal deterrent power is exercised: these are the ruses of the accursed share.

Having said this, the present form of servitude is no longer the – voluntary or involuntary – form of the absence of freedom. It is, rather, that of an excess of freedom in which man, liberated at any price, no longer knows what he is free from, nor why he is free, nor what identity to commit himself to; in which, having all that is around him available for his use, he no longer knows how to make use of himself.

In this sense, the immersion in screens, networks and the technologies of Virtual Reality, with its immense possibilities, has spelled a great stride forward for liberation and has, at the same time, put an end to the question of freedom.

This resiling, in digital manipulation, from care of the self and responsibility – from that portion of freedom and subjectivity to which we lay claim so noisily and which we seek by all possible means to be rid of – is today the easiest solution. To the point where it is the essential task of government forcibly to redistribute responsibility, enjoining everyone to take responsibility for themselves 'freely and fully'.

The political authorities themselves strive constantly to assume an air of responsibility while passing the buck in every possible way (it is, in fact, better to be guilty than responsible, as guilt can always be imputed to some obscure force, whereas, with responsibility, the onus is on you).

Fortunately, there are other, more poetic ways of ridding oneself of freedom – that of gaming, for example, where what is at stake is not a freedom subject to the law, but a sovereignty subject to rules. A more subtle and paradoxical freedom which consists in a rigorous observance, an enchanted form of voluntary servitude that is, as it were, the miraculous combination of master and slave: in gaming no one is free, everyone is both the master and the slave of the game.

Do You Want to be Anyone Else?

Individuality is a recent phenomenon. It is only over the last two centuries that the populations of the civilized countries have demanded the democratic privilege of being individuals.

Before that, they were what they were: slaves, peasants, artisans, men or women, fathers or children – not 'individuals' or 'fully fledged subjects'.

Only with our modern civilization did we find ourselves forcibly inducted into this individual existence.

Of course, we fight to retain this 'inalienable' right, and we are naturally driven to win it and defend it at all costs. We demand this freedom, this autonomy, as a fundamental human right and, at the same time, we are crippled by the responsibility that ends up making us detest ourselves as such.

This is what resounds in the complaint of Job. God asks too much: 'What is man, that thou shouldest magnify him? And that thou shouldest set thy heart upon him? And that thou shouldest visit him every morning, and try him every moment? How long wilt thou not depart from me, nor let me alone till I swallow down my spittle?'[10]

This leaves us subject to a contradictory twofold requirement: to seek an identity by all possible means – by hounding the identities of others or by exploring the networks – and to slough off identity in every possible way, as though it were a burden or a disguise.

It is as though liberty and individuality, from having been a 'natural' state in which one may act freely, had become artificial states, a kind of moral imperative, whose implacable decree makes us hostages to our identities and our own wills.

This is a very particular case of Stockholm Syndrome, since we are here both the terrorist and the hostage. Now, the hostage is by definition the unexchangeable, accursed object you cannot be rid of because you don't know what to do with it.

10. Job 7: 17–19.

The situation is the same for the subject: as hostage to himself, he doesn't know how to exchange himself or be rid of himself.

Being unable to conceive that identity has never existed and that it is merely something we play-act, we fuel this subjective illusion to the point of exhaustion. We wear ourselves out feeding this ghost of a representation of ourselves.

We are overwhelmed by this pretension, this obstinate determination to carry around an identity which it is impossible to exchange (it can be exchanged only for the parallel illusion of an objective reality, in the same metaphysical cycle into which we are locked).

All the grand narratives of our individual consciousness – of freedom, will, identity and responsibility – merely add a useless, even contradictory, over-determination to our actions as they 'occur'. To the effect that we are the cause of them, that they are the doing of our will, that our decisions are the product of our free will, etc.

But our actions do not need this: we can decide and act without there being any need to involve the will and the idea of the will. There is no need to involve the idea of free will to make choices in one's life. Above all, there is no need to involve the idea of subject and its identity in order to exist (it is better, in any case, to involve that of alterity).

These are all useless, like the belief that is superadded to the existence of God (if he exists, he doesn't need it). And so we believe in a free, willed determination of our actions and it gives them a meaning, at the same time as it gives meaning to us – the sense of being the authors of those actions. But this is all a reconstruction, like the reconstruction of the dream narrative.

'A person's actions ... are commonly continuations of his own inner constitution ... the way the magnet bestows form and order on iron filings' (Lichtenberg).[11]

This is the problem Luke Rhinehart sets himself in his novel *The Dice Man*: how are we to slough off this freedom, this ego which is captive to its free will? The solution he finds is that of chance.

Among all the possibilities for shattering the mirror of identity, for freeing beings from the terrorism of the ego, there is the option of surrendering oneself to chance, to the dice, for all one's actions and decisions. No free will any longer, no responsible subject, but merely the play of a random dispersal, an artificial diaspora of the ego.

At bottom, the ego is itself a form of superego: it is the ego we must rid ourselves of, above all.

We must live without reference to a model of identity or a general equivalent.

But the trap with these plural identities, these multiple existences, this devolution on to 'intelligent machines' – dice machines as well as the machines of the networks – is that once the general equivalent has disappeared, all the new possibilities are equivalent to one another and hence cancel each other out in a general indifference. Equivalence is still there, but it is no longer the equivalence of an agency at the top (the ego); it is the equivalence of all the little egos 'liberated' by its disappearance. The erosion of destinies occurs by the very excess of possibilities – as the erosion of knowledge occurs by the very excess of information or sexual erosion by the removal of prohibitions, etc.

11. Fragment E 476.

When, under the banner of identity, existence is so individualized, so atomized ('*atomon*' is the literal equivalent of individual) that its exchange is impossible, the multiplication of existences leads only to a simulacrum of alterity.

To be able to exchange itself for anything or anyone is merely an extreme, desperate form of impossible exchange.

Multiplying identities never produces anything more than all the illusory strategies for decentralizing power: it is pure illusion, pure stratagem.

A fine metaphor of this fractal, proliferating identity is the storyline of the film *Being John Malkovich* (by Spike Jonze) or, more precisely, the moment when Malkovich, by means of a virtual apparatus, goes back into his own skin – until then it was the others who wanted to become Malkovich, this time it is Malkovich who wants to re-enter himself, to become himself at one remove, a meta-Malkovich as it were. It is at this point that he diffracts into countless metastases: by a kind of fantastic image feedback, everyone around him becomes Malkovich. He becomes the universal projection of himself. This is the paroxystic form of identity (here treated with humour).

So it is that everywhere redoubled identity ends in a pure extrapolation of itself. It becomes a special effect which, with the coming of electronic and genetic manipulation, veers towards cloning pure and simple.

It is in the entire machinery of the Virtual and the mental diaspora of the networks today that the fate of *Homo fractalis* is played out: the definitive abdication of his identity and freedom, of his ego and his superego.

In these games of free will and identity, one novel variant is that of the double life.

This is what happens with Romand, who, in order to escape the banality of everyday, provincial life, invents a parallel life for himself and, covering his tracks (to the point where he wipes out his whole family to hide the traces of his 'real' existence), becomes, in his own life, his own stand-in or shadow.[12]

It is by doubling and not in any sense by recourse to dissimulation that Romand imparts a fatal twist to his life. To transfigure insignificance and banality, all that is needed is to turn them into a parallel universe. There is no simulation in all this. All the psychological and sociological explanations of this duplicity and all the categories – lying, cowardice, egoism – to which it is assigned are mere fabrications.

It is not even a question of schizophrenia. The phantom existence into which Romand settles has no meaning, but his home life, his 'normal' life, has no greater meaning. And so, as it were, he substitutes for the insignificance of his real life the even greater insignificance of his double life – transfiguring it in this way by an original form of counter-transference.

And it is this that gave him his energy, the force of inertia that saw him able to bear this clandestine life so long. For, greatly deficient as it may have been, and deadly boring at times, there were extraordinary benefits to be had from it.

There was the possibility of becoming someone else, of existing incognito somewhere else. Of seeing without being seen, of preserving a secret side to oneself, even – indeed,

---

12. The reference is to the celebrated case of Jean-Claude Romand, who, having dropped out of medical school, nonetheless pretended to his family that he had qualified as a doctor and for several years maintained the pretence that he held a high-ranking position within the World Health Organization. For a literary treatment of the case, see Emanuel Carrère, *The Adversary: A True Story of Murder and Deception*. Translated by Linda Coverdale (London: Bloomsbury, 2001).

most importantly – preserving it from one's nearest and dearest.

If Romand was able to survive in this (not even heroic) clandestine state, it was by dint of this secrecy, by dint of something the others had not even an inkling of – real 'insider trading'. This was the price paid for the privilege of playing a game whose rules he alone laid down.

There is the mystery of the invisibility that gave him the strength to spend hours in car parks. The remarkable enjoyment of that monotony that did not even have the charm of solitude.

But there is another mystery: namely, that the others should come, in time, to connive in the illusion. For, unless we assume his wife, parents and children remained silent out of resignation, then their lack of awareness, their ignorance, become as inexplicable as his lingering in the car parks and cafeterias. Except when we see all this as a dual operation, not something got up by a single individual.

Lying, illusion and simulation are always operations in which there is complicity.

The mystified party is always a participant. This is true, indeed, of any relationship: there is no active or passive; there is no individual, there is only the dual.

One cannot therefore test anyone's individual truthfulness or sincerity.

One can no more explain the silence of those around him than Romand's own silence. The deeper he gets into his stratagem, the deeper the others retreat into their absence of curiosity. It is genuinely a conspiracy.

There is no hidden truth. This is what gives the impostor his power. If there were a hidden truth, he could be unmasked, or he could unmask himself.

But we can clearly see throughout the whole story that he cannot, since the imposture is shared. To the point where the fact of wiping out his entire family in the end can, paradoxically, be regarded as a variant of suicide.

For the crime to be perfect, there must be no witnesses for the prosecution, but there must also be no defence witnesses, none who attempt at all costs to explain his act and to unravel this singular conspiracy. To find a moral or social reason is always to betray the secret; but Romand's crime is not so much the murder of his nearest and dearest as the thwarting of any moral and social justification.

In Elia Kazan's film *The Arrangement*, Eddie becomes sick of his own persona in the family and in his work. He therefore resolves to 'suicide' this official Eddie, this conformist version, to find out what his buried double is like, that double of which this 'real' Eddie is merely the empty outer shell. Gradually, then, he strips out all the elements of his conventional life: his job, his wife, his status, his sexuality, and even his father, of whom he rids himself in the end, and the house, which he burns down. Once all the marks of identity are swept away, all the terms of the ordered 'arrangement', what is left? Nothing. He returns to a meaningless conformism, into which he settles like his own shadow – or like the man who has lost his shadow.

The dream of identity ends in indifference.

What can be read between the lines of these stories is that chance and destiny are not to be found elsewhere, in some imaginary decree.

Chance is already present in the unpredictability of ordinary life. There is nothing more unpredictable than any moment of daily life.

All one needs to do is to acknowledge immediately the non-existence of this individual structure, and to recognize that the ego exists only in the showing-through [*transparition*] of the world and all its most insignificant possibilities.

It is no use wondering where freedom or identity lies and what is to be done with them. Human beings are the coming-to-pass of what they are and what they do.

Therein lies the movement of becoming, and what they wanted to be is not an issue; their ideals or free will are not an issue: these are merely retrospective justifications.

At bottom, says Barthes, we are faced with an alternative: either we suppose a real that is entirely permeable to history (to meaning, to the idea, to interpretation, to decision) and we ideologize or, by contrast, we suppose a real that is ultimately impenetrable and irreducible and in that case we poetize.

This would, at any rate, explain the coexistence in everyone of the best and the worst or, in 'criminals' of an absolutely normal behaviour and an unintelligible violence which is itself a thing divided, as though alien to itself, as we see in so much crime reporting. 'He was so gentle, so kind...'

All this is inexplicable in terms of identity and individual will.

This simultaneity of contradictory behaviours merely reflects the entanglement of reality and its disavowal that is our collective horizon today.

Propitious network winds bent their neurones
Toward the instrumental world's virtual rim.[13]

13. This is a pastiche of José-Marie de Hérédia's famous lines: 'Propitious trade-winds bent their antennae/ Towards the western world's mysterious rim' ('The Conquerors', *Cassell's Anthology of French Poetry*, selected and translated by Alan Conder, London, 1950).

The Murder of the Sign

We have abolished the real world.

What world remains, then? The world of signs? Not at all.

We have put paid to the real world and, in the process, done away with that of the sign.

It is the murder of the sign that paves the way for Integral Reality.

It is commonly said that the real has succumbed to the heg-emony of the sign, of images and of the simulacrum – in short, that reality has succumbed to artifice (it is this analysis that underlies the concept of the society of the spectacle).

We must say today, rather, that we have lost the sign and artifice and are left with absolute reality. We have lost the spectacle, alienation, distance, transcendence and abstraction – lost all that still separated us from the advent of Integral Reality, of an immediate, irrevocable realization of the world.

The constellation of the sign disappears with the constella-tion of the real, on the horizon of the Virtual and the digital.

Now, what makes exchange possible if not the abstract trans-cendence of value? What makes the exchange of language possible if not the abstract transcendence of the sign?

It is all these things that are eliminated today, ground to dust.

The same vertiginous deregulation is visited on both value and the sign. Not the real, but the sign and, through it, the whole universe of meaning and communication is undergoing the same deregulation as markets (doubtless it even preceded the deregulation of the world market).

An example: Lascaux.

The original has been closed for many years and it is the simulacrum, Lascaux 2, which the visitors queue for. Most of them no longer even know it is a simulacrum. There's no longer any indication of the original anywhere. This is a sort of prefiguration of the world that awaits us: a perfect copy, which we shall not even know to be a copy. Now, what becomes of the original when the copy is no longer a copy?

This is the ironic dialectic of the simulacrum in the final stage of its disappearance.

Even the original is equally artificial. There is, definitively, no longer any God to recognize his own (in that sense at least, God is indeed dead). So there is a kind of justice here, in the fact that the privileged and the underprivileged both find themselves inhabiting the same artificial world.

Once the original is no longer anything but one allegory among others, in what is, at last, a technically completed world, democracy is fully realized.

Similarly, what becomes of the arbitrary nature of the sign when the referent ceases to be the referent? Now, without the arbitrary nature of the sign, there is no differential function, no language, no symbolic dimension. The sign, ceasing to be a sign, becomes once again a thing among things. That is to say, a thing of total necessity or absolute contingency.

Without instantiation of meaning by the sign, there remains only the fanaticism of language – that fanaticism Rafael Sánchez Ferlosio defines as 'an absolutist inflammation of the signifier'.

This stage is at once the consecration and the end of the political economy of the sign and, one might say, of the golden age of simulation.

Oh happy days, when the simulacrum was still what it was, a game on the fringes of the real and its disappearance, with all the various nuances in the art of disappearing.

This heroic phase is now over. The Virtual – Virtual Reality – ushers in the twilight of the sign and of representation. This concerns the whole universe of the digital, where the binarism of 0 and 1 leaves room only for an operational universe of figures... Integral calculus, integrated circuits. Distance is obliterated, both external distance from the real world and the internal distance specific to the sign.

For the sign is a scene, the scene of representation, of seduction, of language: in language, signs seduce one another beyond meaning and, in their very architecture, signifier and signified are in a dual relation of seduction. And the disappearance of this scene clears the way for a principle of obscenity, a pornographic materialization of everything.

Hence, the direct spectacle of sexual acts that have become a visible performance and an acting-out of the body. No seduction, no representation: merely the integral coding of the body in the visible, where it becomes in fact definitively real, even more than it is really!

One of the variants of this lethal accomplishment, of this acting-out, is the realization of all metaphors – the collapse of the metaphor into the real.

Here, again, we have the phantasm of materializing all that is parable, myth, fable and metaphor.

Romain Gary: 'All humanity's metaphors end up becoming realities. ... I am coming to wonder whether the real aim of science is not a validation of metaphors.'

This same dire fate also befalls dreams, as Machado de Assis prettily relates in his *Dom Casmurro*.

Attempting to recover a dream he lost on waking, the hero enquires of Night, who is at first reluctant to reply, but then admits that the dreams of yesteryear have come to an end. In the past, she, Night, distributed them, since she ruled over the Island of Dreams. But now dreams are born out of the brains of men; they no longer come from elsewhere – from Night or the Gods – they are produced by ourselves out of our memories or our digestions, from anamnesis and needs, from our unconscious or our physiology.

This is the fall of dreams into the psychical domain, 'the fall of the imagination into the psychological swamp' (Hélé Béji). This fall into the psychical domain means, in fact, that dreams no longer have any prophetic value: to do so they would have to originate in a transcendence, the transcendence of night, and come from elsewhere, whereas they are now merely a mode of interaction with oneself.

Prohibitions themselves are no longer transcendent.

Once upon a time they were signified to us from on high by laws that came from a far-off region – perhaps, here again, an Island of Prohibitions, ruled over by a divinity concerned for our fate. But today they too have been internalized; they are produced by the brain.

It is we who produce them; they are secretions of the individual unconscious. They no longer have any grandeur, nor, in the end, do they even have any charm. They either disappear purely and simply (it is forbidden to forbid), or become once again, paradoxically, objects of nostalgia, objects of desire – where once they separated us from the accomplishment of desire.

And, admittedly, all the divinities – of dreams, of prohibitions – are now 'laid off', but it is we who are in mourning for the metaphor.

The abolition of meaning and metaphor can lead also to perverse or poetic effects.

Perverse, the man who sees himself as rubbish and throws himself on to the dustcart shouting 'I'm rubbish!' They pull him out and he jumps in again – he has lost all sense of metaphor.

Perverse and poetic, the woman to whom a man declares that he loves most of all the way she looks at him, and who sends him one of her eyes gift-wrapped.

She too goes beyond the metaphor of the gaze in a cruel act of seduction and counter-transference. The cruel transfiguration of language.

And ironic transfiguration in Harpo Marx's gesture when, to get into the nightclub, he substitutes a real fish for the password 'swordfish'. We are not far in this case from the joke [*Witz*], or from what Freud analyses in the dreamwork in terms of representability (when the word becomes a thing).

There is the same poetic transference in Marcel Duchamp's 'acting-out' when, skipping the stage of the real object and its signification, he sets up his bottle rack as a museum fetish, striking in one go at the classical organization of both the sign and the aesthetic universe.

And it is, indeed, to the more general problem of fetishism that this new twist brings us: after the becoming-sign of the object, the becoming-object of the sign.

In the sexual register, the fetish is no longer a sign but a pure object, meaningless in itself – a banal accessory, but one of absolute value, for which there can be no possible exchange. It is that object and no other.

But this banal singularity means that any object whatever can become a fetish. Its potentiality is total, precisely because it lies beyond any sexual reference or metaphor. It is the perfect object of sex, its perfect realization, insofar as it substitutes for any real sex – just as Virtual Reality substitutes itself for the real world and in that way becomes the universal form of our modern fetishism.

Modern man's immense panoply of information technology has become his true object of (perverse?) desire.

Fetishism being, as the name indicates (*feiticho*), linked to abstraction and artifice, it is all the more radical for the abstraction being total.

If it was possible, in the past, to speak of the fetishism of the commodity, of money, of the simulacrum and the spectacle, that was still a limited fetishism (related to sign-value). There stretches beyond this for us today the world of radical fetishism, linked to the de-signification and limitless operation of the real – to the sign's becoming pure object once again, before or beyond any metaphor.

The same acting-out, the same loss of distance and the same fall into the real threatens thought too, as soon as it crosses the demarcation line which is that of its impossible exchange with truth, as soon as it comes to act out truth.

Thought must at all costs keep itself from reality, from the real projection of ideas and their translation into acts.

The Overman and the Eternal Return are, in this way, visions and they have the sovereignty of a hypothesis. If we try to turn them into acts or *faits accomplis*, they become monstrous and ridiculous.

The same goes for less visionary perspectives, such as biogenetic experimentation on the human species: as a hypothesis, this opens up all kinds of metaphysical and anthropological questions. But if we move from potential mutation to real projection (as Peter Sloterdijk does in his *Menschenpark* project), we lose all philosophical distance; and thought, in mingling with the real course of things, offers merely a false alternative to the operation of the system.

Thought must refrain from instructing, or being instructed by, a future reality, for, in that game, it will always fall into the trap of a system that holds the monopoly of reality.

And this is not a philosophical choice. It is, for thought, a life-and-death question.

The Mental Diaspora of the Networks

Videos, interactive screens, multi-media, the Internet, Virtual Reality: interactivity threatens us on all sides. What was once separated is everywhere merged. Distance is everywhere abolished: between the sexes, between opposite poles, between the stage and the auditorium, between the protagonists of the action, between the subject and the object, between the real and its double.

And this confusion of terms, this collision of poles, means that nowhere is value judgement now possible anywhere any longer: either in art, or in morality or in politics.

By the abolition of distance, of the 'pathos' of distance, everything becomes undecidable.

When an event and the broadcasting of that event in real time are too close together, the event is rendered undecidable and virtual; it is stripped of its historical dimension and removed from memory. We are in a generalized feedback effect.

Wherever a mingling of this kind – a collision of poles – occurs, then the vital tension is discharged. Even in 'reality TV', where, in the live telling of the story, the immediate televisual acting, we see the confusion of existence and its double.

There is no separation any longer, no emptiness, no absence: you enter the screen and the visual image unimpeded. You enter life itself as though walking on to a screen. You slip on your own life like a data suit.

Unlike photography, cinema and painting, where there is a scene and a gaze, the video image, like the computer screen, induces a kind of immersion, a sort of umbilical relation, of 'tactile' interaction, as McLuhan used to say. You enter the fluid substance of the image, possibly to modify it, in the same way as science infiltrates itself into the genome and into the genetic code to transform the body itself.

It is the same with text, with any 'virtual' text (the Internet, word-processing): you work on it like a computer-generated image, which no longer bears any relation to the transcendence of the gaze or of writing. At any rate, as soon as you are in front of the screen, you no longer see the text as a text, but as an image. Now, it is in the strict separation of text and screen, of text and image, that writing is an activity in its own right, never an interaction.

Similarly, it is only with the strict separation of stage and auditorium that the spectator is an actor in his/her own right. Everything today conspires to abolish that separation: the immersion of the spectator in the spectacle, 'living theatre', 'happenings'.

The spectacle becomes user-friendly, interactive. The apogee of spectacle or its end? When everyone is an actor, there is no action any longer, no scene. It's the death of the spectator as such.

The end of the aesthetic illusion.

In fact, everything that was so much trouble to separate, to sex, to transcend, to sublimate and to metamorphose by distance is today being constantly melded together. All that has been wrested from reality we are in the process of realizing by force – there will always be a technique for laying hold of it and making it operational. 'You dreamed it, we made it.' Everything that was so much trouble to destroy, we are today hell-bent on restoring. What we have here, in fact, is an immense reductionism, an immense revisionism.

In the sphere of the Virtual – of the digital, the computer, integral calculus – nothing is representable. It is not a 'scene', and there is neither distance nor a critical or aesthetic gaze: there is total immersion and the countless images that come to us from this media sphere are not of the order of representation, but of decoding and visual consumption. They do not educate us, they inform us. And it is impossible to work back from them to some tangible reality – even a political reality. Even war in this sense is no longer representable, and to the ordeal of war is now added that of the impossibility of representation – in spite of, or because of, the hypervisualization of the event. The war in Iraq and the Gulf War were vivid illustrations of this.

For there to be critical perception and genuine information, the images would have to be different from the war. But they are not (or not any longer): to the routinized violence of war is added the equally routine violence of the images. To the technical virtuality of the war is added the digital virtuality of the images.

If we understand war for what it is today (beyond its political stakes), namely the instrument of a violent acculturation to the world order, then the media and images are part of the Integral Reality of war. They are the subtler instrument of the same homogenization by force.

In this impossibility of reapprehending the world through images and of moving from information to a collective action and will, in this absence of sensibility and mobilization, it isn't apathy or general indifference that's at issue; it is quite simply that the umbilical cord of representation is severed.

77

The screen reflects nothing. It is as though you are behind a two-way mirror: you see the world, but it doesn't see you, it doesn't look at you. Now, you only see things if they are looking at you. The screen screens out any dual relation (any possibility of 'response').

It is this failure of representation which, together with a failure of action, underlies the impossibility of developing an ethics of information, an ethics of images, an ethics of the Virtual and the networks. All attempts in that direction inevitably fail.

All that remains is the mental diaspora of images and the extravagant performance of the medium.

Susan Sontag tells a good story about this pre-eminence of the medium and of images: as she is sitting in front of the television watching the moon landing, the people she is watching with tell her they don't believe it at all. 'But what are you watching, then?' she asks. 'Oh, we're watching television!' Fantastic: they do not see the moon; they see only the screen showing the moon. They do not see the message; they see only the image.

Ultimately, contrary to what Susan Sontag thinks, only intellectuals believe in the ascendancy of meaning; 'people' believe only in the ascendancy of signs. They long ago said goodbye to reality. They have gone over, body and soul, to the spectacular.

What are we to do with an interactive world in which the demarcation line between subject and object is virtually abolished?

That world can no longer either be reflected or represented; it can only be refracted or diffracted now by operations that are, without distinction, operations of brain and screen – the mental operations of a brain that has itself become a screen.

The other side of this Integral Reality is that everything operates in an integrated circuit. In the information media – and in our heads too – the image-feedback dominates, the insistent presence of the monitors – this convolution of things that operate in a loop, that connect back round to themselves like a Klein bottle, that fold back into themselves. Perfect reality, in the sense that everything is verified by adherence to, by confusion with, its own image.

This process assumes its full magnitude in the visual and media world, but also in everyday, individual life, in our acts and thoughts. Such an automatic refraction affects even our perception of the world, sealing everything, as it were, by a focusing on itself.

It is a phenomenon that is particularly marked in the photographic world, where everything is immediately decked out with a context, a culture, a meaning, an idea, disarming any vision and creating a form of blindness condemned by Rafael Sánchez Ferlosio: 'There exists a terrible form of blindness which very few people notice: the blindness that allows you to look and see, but not to see at a stroke without looking. That is how things were before: you didn't look at them, you were happy simply to see them. Everything today is poisoned with duplicity; there is no pure, direct impulse. So, for example, the countryside has become "landscape" or, in other words, a representation of itself…'

In this sense, it is our very perception, our immediate sensibility, that has become aesthetic. Sight, hearing, touch – all our senses have become aesthetic in the worst sense of the term. Any new vision of things can only be the product, then, of a deconstruction of this image-feedback, of a resolution of this counter-transference that blocks our vision, in order to restore the world to its sensory illusoriness (with no feedback and no image feedback).

In the mirror we differentiate ourselves from our image, we enter upon an open form of alienation and of play with it. The mirror, the image, the gaze, the scene – all these things open on to a culture of metaphor.

Whereas in the operation of the Virtual, at a certain level of immersion in the visual machinery, the man/machine distinction no longer holds: the machine is on both sides of the interface. Perhaps you are indeed merely the machine's space now – the human being having become the virtual reality of the machine, its mirror operator.

This has to do with the very essence of the screen. There is no 'through' the screen the way there is a 'through' the looking-glass or mirror. The dimensions of time itself merge there in 'real time'. And, the characteristic of any virtual surface being first of all to be there, to be empty and thus capable of being filled with anything whatever, it is left to you to enter, in real time, into interactivity with the void.

Machines produce only machines. The texts, images, films, speech and programmes which come out of the computer are machine products, and they bear the marks of such products: they are artificially padded-out, face-lifted by the machine; the films are stuffed with special effects, the texts full of *longueurs* and repetitions due to the machine's malicious will to function at all costs (that is *its* passion), and to the operator's fascination with this limitless possibility of functioning.

Hence the wearisome character in films of all this violence and pornographied sexuality, which are merely special effects of violence and sex, no longer even fantasized by humans, but pure machinic violence.

And this explains all these texts that resemble the work of 'intelligent' virtual agents, whose only act is the act of programming.

This has nothing to do with *automatic writing*, which played on the magical telescoping of words and concepts, whereas all we have here is the automatism of programming, an automatic run-through of all the possibilities.

It is this phantasm of the ideal performance of the text or image, the possibility of correcting endlessly, which produce in the 'creative artist' this *vertige* of interactivity with his own object, alongside the anxious *vertige* at not having reached the technological limits of his possibilities.

In fact, it is the (virtual) machine which is speaking you, the machine which is thinking you.

And is there really any possibility of discovering something in cyberspace? The Internet merely simulates a free mental space, a space of freedom and discovery. In fact, it merely offers a multiple but conventional space, in which the operator interacts with known elements, pre-existent sites, established codes. Nothing exists beyond its search parameters. Every question has an anticipated response assigned to it. You are the questioner and, at the same time, the automatic answering device of the machine. Both coder and decoder – you are, in fact, your own terminal.

That is the ecstasy of communication.

There is no 'Other' out there and no final destination. It's any old destination – and any old interactor will do. And so the system goes on, without end and without finality, and its only possibility is that of infinite involution. Hence the comfortable *vertige* of this electronic, computer interaction, which acts like a drug. You can spend your whole life at this, without a break. Drugs themselves are only ever the perfect example of a crazed, closed-circuit interactivity.

People tell you the computer is just a handier, more complex kind of typewriter. But that isn't true. The typewriter is an entirely external object. The page floats free, and so do I. I have a physical relation to writing. I touch the blank or written page with my eyes – something I cannot do with the screen. The computer is a prosthesis. I have a tactile, intersensory relation to it. I become, myself, an ectoplasm of the screen.

And this, no doubt, explains, in this incubation of the virtual image and the brain, the malfunctions which afflict computers, and which are like the failings of one's own body. On the other hand, the fact that priority belongs to the network and not to individuals implies the possibility of hiding, of disappearing into the intangible space of the Virtual, so that you cannot be pinned down anywhere, which resolves all problems of identity, not to mention those of alterity.

So, the attraction of all these virtual machines no doubt derives not so much from the thirst for information and knowledge as from the desire to disappear, and the possibility of dissolving oneself into a phantom conviviality.

A kind of 'high' that takes the place of happiness. But virtuality comes close to happiness only because it surreptitiously removes all reference from it. It gives you everything, but it subtly deprives you of everything at the same time. The subject is, in a sense, realized to perfection, but when realized to perfection, it automatically becomes object, and panic sets in.

However, we must not look on this domination of the Virtual as something inevitable. Above all, we must not take the Virtual for a 'reality' (definitely going too far!) and apply the categories of the real and the rational to it. That is the same misconception as reinterpreting science in the terms of theology, as has been done for centuries, *not seeing that science put an end to theology*. Or interpreting the media in the Marxist terms of alienation, in socio-political terms from ancient history, not seeing that the course of history came to an end with the entry on the scene of the news media and, more generally, that it was all over with reality once the Virtual came on the scene.

However, with the Virtual we find ourselves up against a strange paradox. This is because the Virtual can deny its own reality only at the same time as it denies the reality of all the rest. It is caught up in a game whose rules it does not control (no one controls them!)

The Virtual is not, then, the 'last word'; it is merely the virtual illusion, the illusion of the Virtual.

There is no highest stage of intelligence – and Artificial Intelligence is certainly no such stage.

We have already seen the media revolution being misunderstood when the medium was reduced to a mere instrumental technique. We see here the same misunderstanding of the meaning of the Virtual when it is reduced to an applied technology. People did not see that the irruption of both overturned the very principle of reality. So they speak of the proper use of the Virtual, of an ethics of the Virtual, of virtual 'democracy', without changing anything of the traditional categories.

Now, the specificity of the Virtual is that it constitutes an event *in* the real *against* the real and throws into question all these categories of the real, the social, the political and history – such that the only emergence of any of these things now is virtual.

This is to say that there is no longer any politics now but the virtual (and not a politics *of* the Virtual), no longer any history but the virtual (and not a history *of* the Virtual), no longer any technology but the virtual (and not a technology *of* the Virtual). Not to mention the 'arts of the Virtual' – as though art remained art while playing with the digital and the numeric. Or the economy, which has itself passed over into virtuality, that is to say, into pure speculation.

This upping of the stakes shows that the rationale for the Virtual does not lie within itself, any more than is the case with the economy, and that it constructs itself by headlong flight forward, as a simulation effect, as substitution for the impossible exchange of the world.

Conclusion: from the moment the economic is there for something else, there is no point making endless critiques of it or analysing its transformations.

As soon as the Virtual is there for something else, there is no point enquiring into its principles or purposes, no point being for it or against it.

For the destiny of these things lies elsewhere. And the destiny of the analysis too: everything changes depending on whether you analyse a system by its own logic or in terms of the idea that it is there for something else.

We must have a sense of this illusion of the Virtual somewhere, since, at the same time as we plunge into this machinery and its superficial abysses, *it is as though we viewed it as theatre.* Just as we view news coverage as theatre.

Of news coverage we are the hostages, but we also treat it as spectacle, consume it as spectacle, without regard for its credibility. A latent incredulity and derision prevent us from being totally in the grip of the information media.

It isn't critical consciousness that causes us to distance ourselves from it in this way, but the reflex of no longer wanting to play the game.

Somewhere in us lies a profound desire not to have information and transparency (nor perhaps freedom and democracy

– all this needs looking at again). Towards all these ideals of modernity there is something like a collective form of mental reserve, of innate immunity.

It would be best, then, to pose all these problems in terms other than those of alienation and the unhappy destiny of the subject (which is where all critical analysis ends up).

The unlimited extension of the Virtual itself pushes us towards something like pataphysics, as the science of all that exceeds its own limits, of all that exceeds the laws of physics and metaphysics. The pre-eminently ironic science, corresponding to a state in which things reach a pitch that is simultaneously paroxystic and parodic.

Can we advance the hypothesis that, beyond the critical stage, the heroic stage (which is still that of metaphysics), there is an ironic stage of technology, an ironic stage of history, an ironic stage of value, etc.?

This would free us from the Heideggerian view of technology as the effectuation, and the last stage, of metaphysics; it would free us from all retrospective nostalgia for being, giving us, rather, a gigantic objective irony, a superior intuition of the illusoriness of all this process – which would not be far from the radical post-historical snobbery Alexandre Kojève spoke of.

At the heart of this artificial reality, this Virtual Reality, this irony is perhaps all we have left of the original illusion, which at least preserves us from any temptation one day to possess the truth.

We Are All Agnostics...

When truth and reality were made to take lie-detector tests, they themselves confessed to not believing in truth and reality.

We are all agnostics.

There were those who believed in God and those who did not.

There are those who believe in reality and those who do not.

And then there are the reality agnostics who, though not rejecting it in an absolute sense, reject belief in it: 'Reality (like God in the past) may perhaps exist, but I don't believe in it.'

There is nothing contradictory or absurd in this.

It is the enlightened refusal to let oneself be caught in the trap of a reality that is fetishized in its principle, a reality that is itself caught in the trap of the signs of reality.

Is there such a thing as a naked, original reality, anterior to the signs in which it is made manifest?

Who knows? The self-evidence of reality has a shadow of retrospective doubt hovering over it.

However this may be, the agnostic is not concerned with this hinterworld or this original reality; he confines himself to reality as an unverifiable hypothesis, to signs as signs, behind which might also be hidden the absence of reality. (Their profusion in fact ends up voiding them of their credibility.)

Perhaps the agnostic even prefers signs to reality. Perhaps he prefers this undecidable situation, since you can play with these floating signs and that is not possible with so-called 'objective' reality.

The move from the real to the sign opens up an enormous field of play and uncertainty.

Particularly where the reality of power is concerned.

For if there is, indeed, a risk of anaesthesia and manipulation by signs and images that is to power's advantage, there is the risk that power itself may find itself reduced merely to the signs of power.

This profusion of signs and of what is manifested does, moreover, effect a profound change in the symbolic relation to power.

That relation is based on the unilateral gift (of laws, institutions, work, security, etc.). It is not so much by violence and constraint, but only by this symbolic obligation that power exists. Now, from the point when all that it gives us is signs, our debt to it is infinitely less great. With power distributing nothing but signs to us, we merely give back signs in return, and our servitude is the lighter for it. Admittedly, the enjoyment of immaterial goods is not so great, but this also means we owe little in return and we respond to the airiness of signs with an equal indifference. We can deny power and set it aside by mere incredulity, simply responding to the signs of power with the signs of servitude. This is perhaps what is meant by 'weak thought' (*pensiero debole*).

With Virtual Reality, this process of disinvestment becomes even more radical, and we enter upon a phase of unbinding [*déliaison*], of quasi-total disobligation.

To what in the virtual universe can one feel an obligation?

We are in a state of total agnosticism with regard to the existence of reality, with regard to ends and ultimate meaning – just as the Agnostics were with regard to the existence of God (which may be an asset in terms of technical performance and manipulation – the Agnostics are said to have been very learned and expert in their field).

The question is whether this represents greater freedom or an unprecedented capitulation.

The problem of the symbolic stake is crucial.

Everything is solicitation. Power is a solicitation, meaning is a solicitation, every sign is a solicitation and there cannot but be a reply to that solicitation, either by submission or subversion, by belief or denial of belief.

But the more random and indeterminate is power, the more the signs are meaningless and the more the reply is difficult. Now, power no longer questions us[14] (except in opinion polls where there is no genuine question and hence no possible reply); the signs of exchange no longer question us, except in interaction, communication and information, which are not the site of a dual relation, nor therefore of a genuine reply. Here lies the total abstraction and the source of all domination: in the breakdown of the dual relation.

The strategy of domination is, indeed, to ensure that, through all the techniques of communication, through inescapable, streaming information, there can no longer be any response. It is a domination by signs empty of meaning. But, on the other side, there is an equal indifference and blank resistance.

---

14. '*Le pouvoir*' here might also be rendered as 'those in power', 'the authorities'.

In this way, in a sociality of accelerated circulation but low sign-value, in a game of interaction with neither questions nor responses, power and individuals have no purchase on each other, have no political relationship with each other. This is the price to be paid for flight into the abstraction of the Virtual. But is it a loss?

It seems that it is, today, a collective choice. Perhaps we would rather be dominated by machines than by people, perhaps we prefer an impersonal, automatic domination, a domination by calculation, to domination by a human will? Not to be subject to an alien will, but to an integral calculus that absorbs us and absolves us of any personal responsibility. A minimal definition of freedom perhaps, and one which more resembles a relinquishment, a disillusioned indifference, a mental economy akin to that of machines, which are themselves also entirely irresponsible and which we are coming increasingly to resemble.

This behaviour is not exactly a choice, nor is it a rejection: there is no longer sufficient energy for that. It is a behaviour based on an uncertain negative preference.

Do you want to be free? I would prefer not to...
  Do you want to be represented? I would prefer not to...
  Do you want to be responsible for your own life? I would prefer not to...
  Do you want to be totally happy? I would prefer not to...[15]

---

15. This last paragraph is in English in the original. The allusion is to Herman Melville's story *Bartleby*, in which the eponymous (anti-)hero repeatedly answers 'I would prefer not to', a phrase which is notoriously difficult to render into French.

The Violence Done to the Image

The image also shares the baneful destiny of the sign and the metaphor: the fall into the real.

In itself, the image is bound neither to truth nor to reality; it is appearance and bound to appearance. That is its magical affiliation with the illusion of the world as it is, the affiliation that reminds us that the real is never certain – just as we can never be certain that the worst will happen[16] – and that perhaps the world can do without it, as it can do without the reality principle.

An image, I believe, affects us directly, below the level of representation: at the level of intuition, of perception. At that level, the image is always an absolute surprise. At least it should be.

And in this sense, unfortunately, one may say that images are rare – the power of the image being, most of the time, intercepted by all that we try to make it say.

The image is, most often, dispossessed of its originality, of its own existence as image, and doomed to shameful complicity with the real.

We commonly say that the real has disappeared beneath a welter of signs and images, and it is true that there is a violence of the image. But that violence is substantially offset by the

16. The French saying 'le pire n'est jamais sûr' (the worst is never sure [to happen]) is being alluded to here.

violence done to the image: its exploitation for documentary purposes, as testimony or message, its exploitation for moral, political or promotional ends, or simply for purposes of information...

This is where the destiny of the image comes to an end, both as fateful illusion and vital illusion.

The Iconoclasts of Byzantium smashed images to erase their signification (the visible face of God). While apparently doing the opposite, and in spite of our cult of idols, we are still iconoclasts: we destroy images by overloading them with signification; we kill images with meaning.

Most current images reflect only the misery and violence of the human condition. Yet that misery and violence affect us the less for being over-signified. There is a total misconception in all this.

For its content to affect us, the image must exist by itself; it must impose its original language on us. For there to be transference on to the real, there must be a counter-transference on to the image, and that counter-transference must be resolved.

Today, misery and violence are, through images, becoming a leitmotif of advertising: for example, Toscani incorporates sex and AIDS, war and death into fashion. And why not (the advertising for happiness is no less obscene than that for misfortune)? But on one condition: that the violence of advertising itself be shown, the violence of fashion, the violence of the medium – something advertisers are decidedly incapable of doing. Now, fashion and high society life are themselves, in a sense, a spectacle of death. The world's misery is just as readable in the figure and face of a model as in the skeletal body of an African.

You can read the same cruelty everywhere if you know how to see it.

And indeed, this 'realistic' image does not capture what is, but what should not be – death and misery; it captures that which, from a moral, humanitarian standpoint, ought not to exist (while making a perfectly immoral aesthetic and commercial use of that misery).

Images that ultimately bear witness, behind their alleged 'objectivity', to a deep disavowal of the real, at the same time as a disavowal of the image, which is assigned the task of representing that which does not want to be represented, of violating the real by 'breaking and entering'.

In this sense, most photographs (but media images too, in general, and all that makes up the 'visual') are not true images. They are merely reportage, realist cliché or aesthetic performance, enslaved to all the ideological systems.

At this stage, the image is nothing but an operator of visibility – the medium of an integral visibility that is the pendant to Integral Reality, becoming-real going hand in hand with becoming-visible at all costs: everything must be seen, everything must be visible, and the image is pre-eminently the site of this visibility.

Where the banality of the image meets the banality of life – as in all these 'reality-TV' programmes, such as *Big Brother*, *Loft Story*, etc. – is where this integral visibility begins, where everything is put on view and you realize there no longer is anything to see.

To turn yourself into an image is to expose your daily life, your misfortunes, your desires and your possibilities. It is to have no secrets left. Never to tire of expressing yourself, speaking, communicating. To be readable at every moment, overexposed to the glare of the information media (like the woman who appears live twenty-four hours a day on the Internet, showing the tiniest details of her life).

Is this self-expression the ultimate form of confession that Foucault spoke of? At all events, it is a violence done to the singular being, at the same time as to the image in its singularity.

In *Leaving Las Vegas* (Mike Figgis), you see a young blonde woman calmly peeing while continuing to talk, as indifferent to what she is saying as to what she is doing.

An entirely useless scene, but one that signifies conspicuously that nothing must escape the fade-in/fade-out of reality and fiction; that everything is subject to being put on view; that everything is ready-made for viewing, readied for enjoyment.

This is what transparency means: the forcing of the whole of the real into the orbit of the visual (of representation – but is this still representation? It is exhibitionism, which in fact takes the gaze hostage.)

The obscene is everything that is uselessly, needlessly visible, without desire and without effect – everything that usurps the rare and precious space of appearances.

This is the murder of the image. It lies in this enforced visibility as source of power and control, beyond even the 'panoptical': it is no longer a question of making things visible to an external eye, but of making them transparent to themselves. The power of control is, as it were, internalized, and human beings are no longer victims of images, but rather transform themselves into images.

In Jorge Luis Borges's fable on the 'Fauna of Mirrors', there is the idea that, behind every representation, every image in the mirror, there is a defeated singularity, a conquered enemy who looks like you, who is forced to look like you.[17]

So we may say that behind each image something has disappeared (this indeed is what creates the ambiguous fascination of the image: it is because something in it has disappeared). This was understood by the Iconoclasts, who denounced icons as a way of making God disappear. (Perhaps God himself had chosen to disappear behind the images?)

Today, at all events, it is no longer God, but we ourselves who disappear behind our images. No longer any danger of our image being stolen or our secrecy being violated. We no longer have any secrets. We no longer have anything to hide in this Integral Reality that envelops us.

This is the sign both of our ultimate transparency and our total obscenity.

The ultimate violence done to the image is the violence of the computer-generated image, which emerged *ex nihilo* from numerical calculation and the computer.

There is an end here to the very imagining of the image, to its fundamental 'illusion', since in the process of computer-generation the referent no longer exists and the real itself no longer has cause to come to pass, being produced immediately as Virtual Reality.

There is an end here to that direct image-taking, that presence to a real object in an irrevocable instant, which created the magical illusion of the photograph and made the image a singular event.

17. Borges, 'Fauna of Mirrors', *The Book of Imaginary Beings*. Revised, enlarged and translated by Norman Thomas di Giovanni in collaboration with the author (Harmondsworth: Penguin, 1974), pp. 67–68.

In the virtual image there is no longer anything of that 'punctual' exactitude, of that *punctum* in time (to use Roland Barthes's expression) – that of the old photographic image, which attested that something was there and now no longer is, and hence was testament to a definitive absence freighted with nostalgia.

Digital, numerical production erases the image as *analogon*. It erases the real as something that can be imagined. The photographic act – that moment of disappearance of both subject and object in the same instantaneous confrontation (the shutter release abolishing the world and the gaze just for a moment, a syncope, a *petite mort* that triggers the machinic performance of the image) – disappears in digital, numerical processing.

All this leads inevitably to the death of photography as original medium. It is the essence of photography that disappears with the analogue image. This latter still attested to an ultimate live presence of subject to object. One last reprieve from the dissemination and multiplicity of referentless images, the digital tidal wave that is about to break over us.

The problem of reference was already an almost insoluble problem: where does the real come in? What do we understand by representation? But when, with the Virtual, the referent disappears, when it vanishes into the technical programming of the image, when there is no longer any real world standing over against a light-sensitive film (the same applies with language, which is, as it were, the light-sensitive film of ideas), then there is no longer ultimately any possible representation.

There is a more serious point here. What distinguishes the analogue image from the digital is that within it a form of disappearance is in play, a form of distance, of freezing of the world – that nothingness at the heart of the object which Warhol spoke of.

By contrast, in the digital or, more generally, the computer-generated image there is no longer any negative, no longer anything 'deferred'. In that image nothing dies, nothing disappears. The image is merely the product of an instruction and a programme, aggravated by automatic dissemination from one medium to the other: computer, mobile phone, television screen, etc. – the automaticity of the network matching the automaticity of the construction of the image.

Should we, then, rescue absence and emptiness, should we rescue this nothingness at the heart of the image?

The photographic image is the purest because it simulates neither time nor movement and confines itself to the most rigorous unreality. All the other forms (cinema, video, computer-generated images) are merely attenuated forms of the pure image and its rupture with the real.

The intensity of the image is equal to its denial of the real, to the invention of another scene. To turn an object into an image is to strip it of all its dimensions one by one: weight, relief, aroma, depth, time, continuity and, of course, meaning. It is by dint of this disembodiment that the image assumes this power of fascination, that it becomes a medium of pure objectality, that it becomes transparent to a form of more subtle seduction.

To add back all these dimensions one by one – movement, ideas, meaning, desire – to multi-mediatize the image so as to make things more real, that is to say, better simulated, is a total misconception. And technology itself is caught in its own trap here.

To conceive an image in the pure state, we have to come back to a radically self-evident fact: it is a two-dimensional universe that has its entire perfection in itself and is in no way inferior to the three-dimensional universe of the real and representation or, in some way, the uncompleted phase of that universe.

It is a parallel universe, a depthless other scene, and it is this one dimension fewer that constitutes its specific charm, its genius.

Everything that adds a third dimension to the image, whether it be the dimension of relief, of time and history, of sound and movement, or of ideas and signification; everything that is added to the image, the better to approximate to the real and representation, is a violence that destroys it as parallel universe.

Each supplementary dimension cancels out the preceding ones. The third dimension cancels out the second. As for the fourth dimension, that of the Virtual and the digital, and of Integral Reality, it cancels out all the others – it is a dimensionless hyperspace. It is the hyperspace of our screens where, strictly speaking, the image no longer exists (but the universe of the real and representation no longer exist either).

We must, then, strip away, always strip away, to get back to the image in the pure state. Stripping away brings out the essential point: namely, that the image is more important than what it speaks of, just as language is more important than what it signifies.

There is a haziness about the real.

Reality is not in focus. The bringing into focus of the world would be 'objective reality', that is to say, an adjustment to models of representation – exactly like the focusing of the photographic lens on the object. Fortunately, the world never comes definitively into focus in this way. The lens makes the object move. Or vice versa – but there is movement.

Lichtenberg speaks, in one of his aphorisms, of a tremor: any act, even an exact one, is preceded by a trembling, a haziness of gesture, and it always retains something of it. When this haziness, this tremor, does not exist, when an act is purely operational and is perfectly focused, we are on the verge of madness.

And the true image is the one that accounts for this trembling of the world, whatever the situation or the object, whether it be a war photo or a still life, a landscape or a portrait, an art photo or reportage.

At that stage, the image is something that is part of the world, that is caught up in the same becoming, in the meta morphosis of appearances. A fragment of the hologram of the world, in which each detail is a refraction of the whole.

The peculiar role of photography is not to illustrate the event, but to constitute an event in itself. Logic would demand that the event, the real, occur first and that the image come after to illustrate it. This is, unfortunately, the case most of the time.

A different sequence demands that the event should never exactly take place, that it should remain in a sense a stranger to itself. Something of that strangeness doubtless survives in every event, in every object, in every individual. This is what the image must convey. And, to do so, it must also remain in a sense a stranger to itself; must not conceive itself as medium, not take itself for an image; must remain a fiction and hence echo the unaccountable fiction of the event; must not be caught in its own trap or let itself be imprisoned in the image-feedback.

The worst thing for us is precisely the impossibility of a world without image feed – a world that would not endlessly be laid hold of, captured, filmed and photographed before it has even been seen. A lethal danger for the 'real' world, but also for the image, since where it merely recycles the real and immerses itself in the real there is no longer any image – not, at least, as exception, illusion or parallel universe. In the visual flow submerging us, there is no longer even time for the image to become image.

Can photography exempt itself from this flood of images and restore an original power to them? To do so, the turbulent operation of the world would have to be suspended; the object would have to be caught in that single fantastic moment of first contact when things had not yet noticed we were there, when absence and emptiness had not yet dissipated...

It would, in fact, have to be the world itself that performed the photographic act, as though the world were affording itself the means to appear, quite apart from us.

I dream of an image that would be the automatic writing of the singularity of the world, as dreamt of by the Iconoclasts in the famous Byzantine controversy. The only image they regarded as authentic was one in which the divinity was directly present, as in the veil of the Holy Face[18] – the automatic writing of the divine singularity of the face of Christ without any intervention of the human hand, in a kind of immediate transfer-printing (analogous to the negative of photographic film). By contrast, they violently rejected all the icons produced by human hand

---

18. Also known as the veil of St Veronica.

('cheiropoietic' icons), which, for them, were mere simulacra of the divine.

The photographic act, on the other hand, is, as it were, 'archeiropoietic'. As the automatic writing of light, in which neither the real nor the idea of the real is involved, photography might be said to be, by this automaticity, the prototype of a literalness of the world without intervention of human hand. The world producing itself as radical illusion, as pure trace, with no simulation, no human intervention and, above all, not as truth, for if there is pre-eminently a product of the human mind, that product must be truth and objective reality.

There is a great affectation in giving a meaning to the photographic image. It is making objects strike a pose. And things themselves begin to strike a pose in the light of meaning as soon as they feel the gaze of a subject upon them.

Have we not always nurtured the deep fantasy of a world functioning without us? The poetic temptation to see the world in our absence, free from any human, all-too-human, will?

The intense pleasure of poetic language is to see language functioning on its own, in its materiality, in its literality, without the intermediary of meaning. That is what fascinates us. Similarly in the anagram, in anamorphosis – the 'figure hidden in the carpet'.

Might not photography also function as revelatory, in the dual – technical and metaphysical – sense of the word, of 'the image hidden in the carpet'?

*

The world beyond the polished lenses is more important than the world beyond the seas, and is doubtless exceeded in importance only by the world beyond death (Lichtenberg).

Objects are merely a pretext for light.

If there were no objects, light would circulate endlessly and we would not even be aware of it.

If there were no subjects, thought would circulate infinitely and there would not even be any echo of it in consciousness.

The subject is that upon which thought comes to rest in its infinite circulation, that against which it reflects.

The object is that upon which light comes to rest, that which reflects it.

The photograph is the automatic writing of light.

The silence of the image is equalled only by the silence of the masses and the silence of the desert.

The dream would be to be a photographer without a lens, to move through the world without a camera, in short, to pass beyond photography and see things as though they had themselves passed beyond the image, as though you had already photographed them, but in a past life.

And perhaps we have indeed already passed through the image phase, in the way we pass through different animal phases, the mirror phase being a mere reverberation of all this in our individual lives.

There is no self-portrait.

It is the world which, through the image, produces its own self-portrait and we are allowed there only out of kindness (but the pleasure is shared).

Conversely, every image should be looked at with the same intensity as our images in the mirror.

Photography is always also the veiled message from death in the Samarkand story.[19]
The summoning to a failed meeting with reality ... out of preference, perhaps, for this other world.
Do we not prefer any old parallel universe to the real one?
Any old double life to the one given to us?
There is no finer parallel universe than that of the detail or the fragment.
Freed from the whole and its transcendent ventriloquism, the detail inevitably becomes mysterious.
Every particle wrested from the natural world is in itself an immediate subversion of the real and its wholeness
Like the fragment, it has only to be elliptical.
It has only to be an exception.
Every singular image can be reckoned exceptional.
And it puts an end to all the others.

A lens so subtle that it would capture only those who are really there and not those pretending to be there or those so absent from themselves that the film would be insensitive to them, as with ectoplasms and vampires.

19. Baudrillard has referred to this story on many occasions. In one of the variants, it runs as follows: 'On the town square a soldier sees death beckoning to him. He takes fright, goes to see the king and says, "Death has beckoned to me, I am going to flee as far away as possible, I am fleeing to Samarkand." The king commands that death be sent to him, to explain why it has terrified his captain. And death tells him, "I didn't want to frighten him. I simply wanted to remind him we had an appointment tonight – in Samarkand".' *Passwords*. Translated by Chris Turner (London: Verso, 2003), p. 68.

At any rate, the lens simultaneously captures the way we are there and the way we are no longer there.

This is why, before the eye of the camera, we act dead in our innermost being, as God does before the proofs of his existence.

Everything in us crystallizes negatively before the material imagining of our presence.

The focusing is done on absence and not on presence. The singularity is that of an object, an image, a fragment, a thought which, to use Mark Rothko's fine expression, 'opens and closes up simultaneously in all directions'.

To wrest the real from the reality principle.

To wrest the image from the representation principle.

To rediscover the image as point of convergence between the light from the object and the light from the gaze.

Contemporary Art: Art Contemporary with Itself

The adventure of modern art is over. Contemporary art is contemporary only with itself. It no longer knows any transcendence either towards past or future; its only reality is that of its operation in real time and its confusion with that reality.

Nothing now distinguishes it from the technical, promotional, media, digital operation. There is no transcendence, no divergence any more, nothing of another scene: merely a specular play with the contemporary world as it takes place. It is in this that contemporary art is worthless: between it and the world, there is a zero-sum equation.

Quite apart from that shameful complicity in which creators and consumers commune wordlessly in the examination of strange, inexplicable objects that refer only to themselves and to the idea of art, the true conspiracy lies in this complicity that art forges with itself, its collusion with the real, through which it becomes complicit in that Integral Reality, of which it is now merely the image-feedback.

There is no longer any differential of art. There is only the integral calculus of reality. Art is now merely an idea prostituted in its realization.

Modernity was the golden age of a deconstruction of reality into its simple elements, of a detailed analytics, first of impressionism, then of abstraction, experimentally open to all the aspects of perception, of sensibility, of the structure of the object and the dismemberment of forms.

The paradox of abstraction is that, by 'liberating' the object from the constraints of the figural to yield it up to the pure play of form, it shackled it to an idea of a hidden structure, of an objectivity more rigorous and radical than that of resemblance. It sought to set aside the mask of resemblance and of the figure in order to accede to the analytic truth of the object. Under the banner of abstraction, we moved paradoxically towards more reality, towards an unveiling of the 'elementary structures' of objectality, that is to say, towards something more real than the real.

Conversely, under the banner of a general aestheticization, art invaded the whole field of reality.

The end of this history saw the banality of art merge with the banality of the real world – Duchamp's act, with its automatic transference of the object, being the inaugural (and ironic) gesture in this process. The transference of all reality into aesthetics, which has become one of the dimensions of generalized exchange...

All this under the banner of a simultaneous liberation of art and the real world.

This 'liberation' has in fact consisted in indexing the two to each other – a chiasmus lethal to both.

The transference of art, become a useless function, into a reality that is now integral, since it has absorbed everything that denied, exceeded or transfigured it. The impossible exchange of this Integral Reality for anything else whatever. Given this, it can only exchange itself for itself or, in other words, repeat itself *ad infinitum.*

What could miraculously reassure us today about the essence of art? Art is quite simply what is at issue in the world of art, in that desperately self-obsessed artistic community. The 'creative' act doubles up on itself and is now nothing more than a sign of its own operation – the painter's true subject is no longer what he paints but the very fact that he paints. He paints the fact that he paints. At least in that way the idea of art remains intact.

This is merely one of the sides of the conspiracy.

The other side is that of the spectator who, for want of understanding anything whatever most of the time, consumes his own culture at one remove. He literally consumes the fact that he understands nothing and that there is no necessity in all this except the imperative of culture, of being a part of the integrated circuit of culture. But culture is itself merely an epiphenomenon of global circulation.

The idea of art has become rarefied and minimal, leading ultimately to conceptual art, where it ends in the non-exhibition of non-works in non-galleries – the apotheosis of art as non-event. As a corollary, the consumer circulates in all this in order to experience his non-enjoyment of the works.

At the extreme point of a conceptual, minimalist logic, art ought quite simply to fade away. At that point, it would doubtless become what it is: a false problem, and every aesthetic theory would be a false solution.

And yet it is the case that there is all the more need to speak about it because there is nothing to say. The movement of the democratization of art has paradoxically merely strengthened the privileged status of the *idea* of art, culminating in this banal tautology of 'art is art', it being possible for everything to find its place in this circular definition.

As Marshall McLuhan has it, 'We have now become aware of the possibility of arranging the entire human environment as a work of art.'[20]

The revolutionary idea of contemporary art was that any object, any detail or fragment of the material world, could exert the same strange attraction and pose the same insoluble questions as were reserved in the past for a few rare aristocratic forms known as works of art.

That is where true democracy lay: not in the accession of everyone to aesthetic enjoyment, but in the transaesthetic advent of a world in which every object would, without distinction, have its fifteen minutes of fame (particularly objects without distinction). All objects are equivalent, everything is a work of genius. With, as a corollary, the transformation of art and of the work itself into an object, without illusion or transcendence, a purely conceptual acting-out, generative of deconstructed objects which deconstruct us in their turn.

No longer any face, any gaze, any human countenance or body in all this – organs without bodies, flows, molecules, the fractal. The relation to the 'artwork' is of the order of contamination, of contagion: you hook up to it, absorb or immerse yourself in it, exactly as in flows and networks. Metonymic sequence, chain reaction.

No longer any real object in all this: in the ready-made it is no longer the object that's there, but the idea of the object, and we no longer find pleasure here in art, but in the idea of art. We are wholly in ideology.

And, ultimately, the twofold curse of modern and contemporary art is summed up in the 'ready-made': the curse of an

20. In English in the original.

immersion in the real and banality, and that of a conceptual absorption in the idea of art.

'...that absurd sculpture by Picasso, with its stalks and leaves of metal; neither wings, nor victory, just a testimony, a vestige – the idea, nothing more, of a work of art. Very similar to the other ideas and vestiges that inspire our existence – not apples, but the idea, the reconstruction by the pomologist of what apples used to be – not ice-cream, but the idea, the memory of something delicious, made from substitutes, from starch, glucose and other chemicals – not sex, but the idea or evocation of sex – the same with love, belief, thought and the rest...'[21]

Art, in its form, signifies nothing. It is merely a sign pointing towards absence.

But what becomes of this perspective of emptiness and absence in a contemporary universe that is already totally emptied of its meaning and reality?

Art can now only align itself with the general insignificance and indifference. It no longer has any privileged status. It no longer has any other final destination than this fluid universe of communication, the networks and interaction.

Transmitter and receiver merging in the same loop: all transmitters, all receivers. Each subject interacting with itself, doomed to express itself without any longer having time to listen to the other.

The Net and the networks clearly increase this possibility of transmitting for oneself in a closed circuit, everyone going

21. This passage is cited from an unidentified work by Saul Bellow, and I have not been able to trace the original. As a result, I can only offer here a retranslation of the French.

at it with their virtual performances and contributing to the general asphyxia.

This is why, where art is concerned, the most interesting thing would be to infiltrate the spongiform encephalon of the modern spectator. For this is where the mystery lies today: in the brain of the receiver, at the nerve centre of this servility before 'works of art'. What is the secret of it? In the complicity between the mortification 'creative artists' inflict on objects and themselves, and the mortification consumers inflict on themselves and their mental faculties.

Tolerance for the worst of things has clearly increased considerably as a function of this general state of complicity.

Interface and performance – these are the two current leitmotifs.

In performance, all the forms of expression merge – the plastic arts, photography, video, installation, the interactive screen. This vertical and horizontal, aesthetic and commercial diversification is henceforth part of the work, the original core of which cannot be located.

A (non-)event like *The Matrix* illustrates this perfectly: this is the very archetype of the global installation, of the total global fact: not just the film, which is, in a way, the alibi, but the spin-offs, the simultaneous projection at all points of the globe and the millions of spectators themselves who are inextricably part of it. We are all, from a global, interactive point of view, the actors in this total global fact.

Photography has the selfsame problem when we undertake to multi-mediatize it by adding to it all the resources of montage, collage, the digital and CGI, etc. This opening-up to the infinite, this deregulation, is, literally, the death of photography by its elevation to the stage of performance.

In this universal mix, each register loses its specificity – just as each individual loses his sovereignty in interaction and the networks – just as the real and the image, art and reality lose their respective energy by ceasing to be differential poles.

Since the nineteenth century, it has been art's claim that it is useless. It has prided itself on this (which was not the case in classical art, where, in a world that was not yet either real or objective, the question of usefulness did not even arise).

Extending this principle, it is enough to elevate any object to uselessness to turn it into a work of art. This is precisely what the 'ready-made' does, when it simply withdraws an object from its function, without changing it in any way, and thereby turns it into a gallery piece. It is enough to turn the real itself into a useless function to make it an art object, prey to the devouring aesthetic of banality.

Similarly, old objects, being obsolete and hence useless, automatically acquire an aesthetic aura. Their being distant from us in time is the equivalent of Duchamp's artistic act; they too become 'ready-mades', nostalgic vestiges resuscitated in our museum universe.

We might extrapolate this aesthetic transfiguration to the whole of material production. As soon as it reaches a threshold where it is no longer exchanged in terms of social wealth, it becomes something like a giant Surrealist object, in the grip of a devouring aesthetic, and everywhere takes its place in a kind of virtual museum. And so we have the museification, like a 'ready-made', of the whole technical environment in the form of industrial wasteland.

The logic of uselessness could not but lead contemporary art to a predilection for waste, which is itself useless by definition. Through waste, the figuration of waste, the obsession with waste, art fiercely proclaims its uselessness. It demonstrates its non-use-value, its non-exchange-value at the same time as selling itself very dear.

There is a misconception here. *Uselessness has no value in itself.* It is a secondary symptom and, by sacrificing its aims to this negative quality, art goes completely off track, into a gratuitousness that is itself useless. It is the same scenario, more or less, as that of nullity, of the claim to non-meaning, insignificance and banality, which attests to a redoubled aesthetic pretension.

Anti-art strives, in all its forms, to escape the aesthetic dimension. But since the 'ready-made' has annexed banality itself, all that is finished. The innocence of non-meaning, of the non-figurative, of abjection and dissidence, is finished.

All these things, which contemporary art would like to be, or return to, merely reinforce the inexorably aesthetic character of this anti-art.

Art has always denied itself. But once it did so through excess, thrilling to the play of its disappearance. Today it denies itself by default – worse, it denies its own death.

It immerses itself in reality, instead of being the agent of the symbolic murder of that same reality, instead of being the magical operator of its disappearance.

And the paradox is that the closer it gets to this phenomenal confusion, this nullity as art, the greater credit and value it is accorded, to the extent that, to paraphrase Canetti, we have reached a point where nothing is beautiful or ugly any more; we passed that point without realizing it and, since we cannot get back to that blind spot, we can only persevere in the current destruction of art.

Lastly, what purpose does this useless function serve?

From what, by its very uselessness, does it deliver us?

Like politicians, who deliver us from the wearisome responsibility of power, contemporary art, by its incoherent artifice, delivers us from the ascendancy of meaning by providing us with the spectacle of non-sense. This explains its proliferation: independently of any aesthetic value, it is assured of prospering by dint of its very insignificance and emptiness. Just as the politician endures in the absence of any representativeness or credibility.

So art and the art market flourish precisely in proportion to their decay: they are the modern charnel-houses of culture and the simulacrum.

It is absurd, then, to say that contemporary art is worthless and that there's no point to it, since that is its vital function: to illustrate our uselessness and absurdity. Or, more accurately, to make that decay its stock in trade, while exorcizing it as spectacle.

If, as some have proposed, the function of art was to make life more interesting than art, then we have to give up that illusion. One gets the impression that a large part of current art participates in an enterprise of deterrence, a work of mourning for the image and the imaginary, a mostly failed work of aesthetic mourning that leads to a general melancholia of the artistic sphere, which seems to survive its own demise by recycling its history and its relics.

But neither art nor aesthetics is alone in being doomed to this melancholy destiny of living not beyond their means, but beyond their ends.

Our capacity for degradation is infinite, and so long as we have not brought out all the crime that is potentially within us, our journey will not be at an end.

Guido Ceronetti

If man must reach the outermost bounds of his possibilities, then he must also go so far as to destroy himself. For that possibility is neither the least, nor the least glorious.

Saul Bellow

Virtuality and Events

Two images: that of the bronze technocrat, bent over his brief-case, sitting on a bench at the foot of the Twin Towers, or, rather, shrouded in the dust of the collapsed towers like one of those bodies found in the ruins of Pompeii. He was, so to speak, the signature of the event, the pathetic ghost of a global power hit by an unforeseeable catastrophe.

Another figure: that of that artist working in his studio in the Towers on a sculpture of himself – his body pierced with aeroplanes – intended to stand on the plaza of the World Trade Centre like a modern Saint Sebastian.[22]

He was still working on it on the morning of 11 September when he was swept away, together with his sculpture, by the very event the work prefigured. The supreme consecration for a work of art: to be realized by the very event that destroys it.

Two allegories of an exceptional, earth-shattering event, cutting at a stroke through the monotony of a declared end of history. The only event worthy of the name, contrasting starkly with the non-event to which we are condemned by the hegemony of a world order nothing must disturb.

At this present stage of a networking of all functions – of the body, of time, of language – of a drip-feeding of all minds, the slightest event is a threat; even history is a threat.

22. The works referred to here are by J. Seward Johnson and the late Michael Richards, respectively.

It is going to be necessary, then, to invent a security system that prevents any event whatever from occurring. A whole strategy of deterrence that does service today for a global strategy.

Steven Spielberg's recent film, *Minority Report*, provides an illustration of such a system. On the basis of brains endowed with a gift of pre-cognition (the 'precogs'), who identify imminent crimes before they occur, squads of police (the 'precrimes') intercept and neutralize the criminal before he has committed his crime. There is a variant in the film *Dead Zone* (directed by David Cronenberg): the hero, who, following a serious accident, is also endowed with powers of divination, ends up killing a politician whose future destiny as a war criminal he foresees. This is the scenario of the Iraq war too: the crime is nipped in the bud on the strength of an act that has not taken place (Saddam's use of weapons of mass destruction). The question is clearly whether the crime would really have taken place. But we shall never know. What we have here, then, is the real repression of a virtual crime. Extrapolating from this, we can see looming beyond the war a systematic de-programming not only of all crime, but of anything that might disturb the order of things, the policed order of the planet. This is what 'political' power comes down to today. It is no longer driven by any positive will; it is merely a negative power of deterrence, of public health, of security policing, immunity policing, prophylaxis.

This strategy is directed not only at the future, but also at past events – for example, at that of 11 September, where it attempts, by war in Afghanistan and Iraq, to erase the humiliation. This is why this war is at bottom a delusion, a virtual event, a 'non-event'. Bereft of any objective or finality of its own, it merely takes the form of an incantation, an exorcism. This is also why it is interminable, for there will never be any end to conjuring away such an event. It is said to be preventive, but it is in fact retrospective, its aim being to defuse the terrorist event of 11 September, the shadow of which hovers over the whole strategy of planetary control. Erasure of the event, erasure of the enemy, erasure of death: in the insistence on 'zero casualties' we see the very same imperative as applies in this obsession with security.[23]

The aim of this world order is the definitive non-occurrence of events. It is, in a sense, the end of history, not on the basis of a democratic fulfilment, as Fukuyama has it, but on the basis of preventive terror, of a counter-terror that puts an end to any possible events. A terror which the power exerting it ends up exerting on itself under the banner of security.

There is a fierce irony here: the irony of an anti-terrorist world system that ends up internalizing terror, inflicting it on itself and emptying itself of any political substance – and going so far as to turn on its own population.

Is this a remnant of the Cold War and the balance of terror? But this time it's a deterrence without cold war, a terror without balance. Or rather it is a universal cold war, ground into the tiniest interstices of social and political life.

This headlong rush by power into its own trap reached dramatic extremes in the Moscow theatre episode, when the hostages and the terrorists were jumbled together in the same

---

23. The French terms 'la sécurité' and 'l'insécurité' advert more clearly than their English cognates to the debate on what is colloquially known in English as 'law and order'.

massacre. Exactly as in Mad Cow Disease: you kill the whole herd as a precautionary measure – God will recognize his own. Or as in Stockholm Syndrome: being jumbled together in death makes them virtually partners in crime (it is the same in *Minority Report*: the fact that the police seize the presumptive criminal before he has done anything proves *a posteriori* that he cannot be innocent).

And this is, in fact, the truth of the situation: the fact is that, one way or another, populations themselves are a terrorist threat to the authorities. And it is the authorities themselves who, by repression, unwittingly set the seal on this complicity. The equivalence in repression shows that we are all potentially the hostages of the authorities.

By extension, we can hypothesize a coalition of all governments against all populations – we have had a foretaste of this with the war in Iraq, since it was able to take place in defiance of world opinion, with the more or less disguised assent of all governments. And if the world-wide demonstrations against war may have produced the illusion of a possible counter-power, they demonstrated above all the political insignificance of this 'international community' by comparison with American *Realpolitik*.

We are dealing henceforth with the exercise of power in the pure state with no concern for sovereignty or representation; with the Integral Reality of a negative power. So long as it derives its sovereignty from representation, so long as a form of political reason exists, power can find its equilibrium – it can, at any rate, be combated and contested. But the eclipsing of that sovereignty leaves an unbridled power, with nothing standing against it, a savage power (with a savagery that is no longer natural, but technical). And which, in a strangely roundabout way, might be said to get back to something like primitive societies, which, not knowing power, were, according to Claude Lévi-Strauss, societies without history. What if we, the present global society, were once again, in the shadow of this integral power, to become a society without history?

But this Integral Reality of power is also its end. A power that is no longer based on anything other than the prevention and policing of events, which no longer has any political will but the will to dispel ghosts, itself becomes ghostly and vulnerable. Its virtual power – its programming power in terms of software and the like – is total, but as a result it can no longer bring itself into play, except against itself, by all kinds of internal failures. At the height of its mastery, it can now only lose face.
    This is, literally, the 'Hell of Power'.

The policing of events is essentially carried out by information itself.[24] Information represents the most effective machinery for de-realizing history. Just as political economy is a gigantic machinery for producing value, for producing signs of wealth, but not wealth itself, so the whole system of information is an immense machine for producing the event as sign, as an exchangeable value on the universal market of ideology, of spectacle, of catastrophe, etc. – in short, for producing a non-event. The abstraction of information is the same as the abstraction of the economy. And, as all commodities, thanks to this abstraction of value, are exchangeable one with another, so all events become substitutable one for another in the cultural information market. The singularity of the event,

---

24. 'L'information' in French has a broader range of reference than in English, denoting both information in the English sense, where it connects with information technology (l'informatique), and also news coverage in a general sense (cf. la presse d'information: the newspapers).

irreducible to its coded transcription and its staging, which is what quite simply constitutes an event, is lost.

We are passing into a realm where events no longer truly take place, by dint of their very production and dissemination in 'real time' – where they become lost in the void of news and information.

The sphere of information is like a space where, after having emptied events of their substance, an artificial gravity is re-created and they are put back in orbit in 'real time' – where, having shorn them of historical vitality, they are re-projected on to the transpolitical stage of information.

The non-event is not when nothing happens.

It is, rather, the realm of perpetual change, of a ceaseless updating, of an incessant succession in real time, which produces this general equivalence, this indifference, this banality that characterizes the zero degree of the event.

A perpetual escalation that is also the escalation of growth – or of fashion, which is pre-eminently the field of compulsive change and built-in obsolescence. The ascendancy of models gives rise to a culture of difference that puts an end to any historical continuity. Instead of unfolding as part of a history, things have begun to succeed each other in the void. A profusion of language and images before which we are defenceless, reduced to the same powerlessness, to the same paralysis as we might show on the approach of war.

It isn't a question of disinformation or brainwashing. It was a naïve error on the part of the FBI to attempt to create a Disinformation Agency for purposes of managed manipulation – a wholly useless undertaking, since disinformation comes from the very profusion of information, from its incantation, its looped repetition, which creates an empty perceptual field, a space shattered as though by a neutron bomb or by one of those devices that sucks in all the oxygen from the area of impact. It's a space where everything is pre-neutralized, including war, by the precession of images and commentaries, but this is perhaps because there is at bottom nothing to say about something that unfolds, like this war, to a relentless scenario, without a glimmer of uncertainty regarding the final outcome.

It is in the sphere of the media that we most clearly see the event short-circuited by its immediate image-feedback.

Information, news coverage, is always already there. When there are catastrophes, the reporters and photo-journalists are there before the emergency services. If they could be, they would be there before the catastrophe, the best thing being to invent or cause the event so as to be first with the news.

This kind of speculation reached a high point with the Pentagon's initiative of creating a 'futures market in events', a stock market of prices for terrorist attacks or catastrophes. You bet on the probable occurrence of such events against those who don't believe they'll happen.

This speculative market is intended to operate like the market in soya or sugar. You might speculate on the number of AIDS victims in Africa or on the probability that the San Andreas Fault will give way (the Pentagon's initiative is said to derive from the fact that they credit the free market in speculation with better forecasting powers than the secret services).

Of course it is merely a step from here to insider trading: betting on the event before you cause it is still the surest way (they say Bin Laden did this, speculating on TWA shares before 11 September). It's like taking out life insurance on your wife before you murder her.

There's a great difference between the event that happens (happened) in historical time and the event that happens in the real time of information.

To the pure management of flows and markets under the banner of planetary deregulation, there corresponds the 'global' event – or rather the globalized non-event: the French victory in the World Cup, the year 2000, the death of Diana, *The Matrix*, etc.

Whether or not these events are manufactured, they are orchestrated by the silent epidemic of the information networks. Fake events.[25]

François de Bernard analyses the war in Iraq this way, as a pure transcription of film theory and practice. What we are watching as we sit paralysed in our fold-down seats isn't '*like* a film'; it *is* a film. With a script, a screenplay, that has to be followed unswervingly.

The casting and the technical and financial resources have all been meticulously scheduled: these are professionals at work. Including control of the distribution channels. In the end, operational war becomes an enormous special effect; cinema becomes the paradigm of warfare, and we imagine it as 'real', whereas it is merely the mirror of its cinematic being.

The virtuality of war is not, then, a metaphor. It is the literal passage from reality into fiction, or rather the immediate metamorphosis of the real into fiction. The real is now merely the asymptotic horizon of the Virtual.

And it isn't just the reality of the real that's at issue in all this, but the reality of cinema. It's a little like Disneyland: the

---

25. 'Fake events' in English in the original.

theme parks are now merely an alibi – masking the fact that the whole context of life has been disneyfied.

It's the same with the cinema: the films produced today are merely the visible allegory of the cinematic form that has taken over everything – social and political life, the landscape, war, etc. – the form of life totally scripted for the screen. This is no doubt why cinema is disappearing: because it has passed into reality. Reality is disappearing at the hands of the cinema and cinema is disappearing at the hands of reality. A lethal transfusion in which each loses its specificity.

If we view history as a film – which it has become in spite of us – then the truth of information consists in the post-synchronization, dubbing and sub-titling of the film of history.

In the former West Germany they are going to build a theme park where the décor and ambience of the now defunct East will be re-created (*Ost*-algia as a form of nostalgia). A whole society memorialized in this way in its own lifetime (it has not completely disappeared).

So the simulacrum does not merely telescope actuality, but gives the impression that the 'Real' will soon eventuate only in 'real time' without even passing through the present and history.

As a result, history becomes once again for us an object of nostalgia, and a desire for history, for rehabilitation, for sites of memory, can be seen flourishing everywhere, as though, even as we suffer it, we are striving to fuel this same end of history.

History too is operating beyond its own end.

There was a definition of the historical event and the French Revolution was its model. The very concepts of event and history date really from that point. The event could be analysed as the high point in a continuous unfolding and its discontinuity was itself part of an overall dialectic.

It is not that way at all now, with the rise of a world order exclusive of all ideology and exclusively concerned with the circulation of flows and networks. In that generalized circulation, all the objectives and values of the Enlightenment are lost, even though they were at its origin. For there was once an idea, an ideal, an imaginary of modernity, but these have all disappeared in the exacerbation of growth.

It is the same with history as it is with reality.

There was a reality principle. Then the principle disappeared and reality, freed from its principle, continues to run on out of sheer inertia. It develops exponentially, it becomes Integral Reality, which no longer has either principle or end, but is content merely to realize all possibilities integrally. It has devoured its own utopia. It operates beyond its own end.

But the end of history is not the last word on history.

For, against this background of perpetual non-events, there looms another species of event. Ruptural events, unforeseeable events, unclassifiable in terms of history, outside of historical reason, events which occur against their own image, against their own simulacrum. Events that break the tedious sequence of current events as relayed by the media, but which are not, for all that, a reappearance of history or a Real irrupting in the heart of the Virtual (as has been said of 11 September). They do not constitute events *in* history, but *beyond* history, beyond its end; they constitute events in a system that has put an end to history. They are the internal convulsion of history. And, as a result, they appear inspired by some power of evil, appear no longer the bearers of a constructive disorder, but of an absolute disorder.

Indecipherable in their singularity, they are the equivalent in excess of a system that is itself indecipherable in its extension and its headlong charge.

In the New World Order there are no longer any revolutions, there are now only convulsions. As in an allegedly perfect mechanism, a system that is too well integrated, there are no longer any crises, but malfunctions, faults, breakdowns, aneurysmal ruptures.

Yet events are not the same as accidents.

The accident is merely a symptom, an episodic dysfunction, a fault in the technical (or natural) order that can possibly be prevented. This is what all the current politics of risk and prevention is about.

The event, for its part, is counter-offensive and much stranger in inspiration: into any system at its peak, at its point of perfection, it reintroduces internal negativity and death. It is a form of the turning of power against itself, as if, alongside the ingredients of its power, every system secretly nourished an evil spirit that would ensure that system were overturned.

It is in this sense that, unlike accidents, such events cannot be predicted and they form no part of any set of probabilities.

The analysis of revolution and the spectre of communism by Marx offers plenty of analogies with the current situation. He too made the proletariat the historic agent of the end of capital – its evil spirit, so to speak, since, with the rise of the proletariat, capital fomented the internal virus of its own destruction.

There is, however, a radical difference between the spectre of communism and that of terrorism. For capital's great trick was to transform the agent of disintegration it carried within it into a visible enemy, a class adversary, and thus, beyond economic exploitation, to change this historic movement into a dynamic of reintegration leading to a more advanced stage of capital.

Terrorism operates at a higher level of radicalism: it is not a subject of history; it is an elusive enemy. And if the class struggle generated historical events, terrorism generates another type of event. Global power (which is no longer quite the same as capital) finds itself here in direct confrontation with itself. It is now left to deal not with the spectre of communism, but with its own spectre.

The end of revolutions (and of history in general) is not, then, in any sense a victory for global power. It might rather be said to be a fateful sign for it.

History was our strong hypothesis, the hypothesis of maximum intensity.

Change, for its part, corresponds to a minimum intensity – it is where everything merely follows everything else and cancels it out, to the point of re-creating total immobilism: the impression, amid the whirl of current events, that nothing changes.

Generalized exchange – the exchange of flows, of networks, of universal communication – leads, beyond a critical threshold we passed long ago, to its own denial, which is no longer then a mere crisis of growth, but a catastrophe, a violent involution, which can be felt today in what might be called the 'tendency of the rate of reality to fall' (similarly, the profusion of information corresponds to a tendency of the rate of knowledge to fall).

Zero degree of value in total equivalence.

Globalization believed it would succeed in the neutralization of all conflicts and would move towards a *faultless* order. But it is, in fact, an order *by default*: everything is equivalent to everything else in a zero-sum equation. Gone is the dialectic, the play of thesis and antithesis resolving itself in synthesis. The opposing terms now cancel each other out in a levelling of all conflict. But this neutralization is, in its turn, never definitive, since, at the same time as all dialectical resolution disappears, the extremes come to the fore.

No longer a question of a history in progress, of a directive schema or of regulation by crisis. No longer any rational continuity or dialectic of conflicts, but a sharing of extremes. Once the universal has been crushed by the power of the global and the logic of history obliterated by the dizzying whirl of change, there remains only a face-off between virtual omnipotence and those fiercely opposed to it.

Hence the antagonism between global power and terrorism – the present confrontation between American hegemony and Islamist terrorism being merely the visible current twist in this duel between an Integral Reality of power and integral rejection of that same power.

There is no possible reconciliation; there never will be an armistice between the antagonistic forces, nor any possibility of an integral order.

Never any armistice of thought either, which resists it fiercely, or an armistice of events in this sense: at most, events go on strike for a time, then suddenly burst through again.

This is, in a way, reassuring: though it cannot be dismantled, the Empire of Good is also doomed to perpetual failure.

We must retain for the event its radical definition and its impact in the imagination. It is characterized entirely, in a paradoxical way, by its uncanniness, its troubling strangeness – it is the irruption of something improbable and impossible – and by its troubling familiarity: from the outset it seems totally self-explanatory, as though predestined, as though it could not but take place.

There is something here that seems to come from elsewhere, something fateful that nothing can prevent. It is for this reason, both complex and contradictory, that it mobilizes the imagination with such force. It breaks the continuity of things and, at the same time, makes its entry into the real with stupefying ease.

Bergson felt the event of the First World War this way. Before it broke out, it appeared both possible and impossible (the similarity with the suspense surrounding the Iraq war is total), and at the same time he experienced a sense of stupefaction at the ease with which such a fearful eventuality could pass from the abstract to the concrete, from the virtual to the real.

We see the same paradox again in the mix of jubilation and terror that characterized, in a more or less unspoken way, the event of 11 September.

It is the feeling that seizes us when faced with the occurrence of *something that happens without having been possible.*

In the normal course of events, things first have to be possible and can only actualize themselves afterwards. This is the logical, chronological order. But they are not, in that case, events in the strong sense.

This is the case with the Iraq war, which has been so predicted, programmed, anticipated, prescribed and modelled that it has exhausted all its possibilities before even taking place. There is no longer anything of the event in it. There is no longer anything in it of that sense of exaltation and horror felt in the radical event of 11 September, which resembles the sense of the sublime spoken of by Kant. The non-event of the war leaves merely a sense of mystification and nausea.

It is here we must introduce something like a metaphysics of the event, indications of which we find once again in Bergson. Asked if it was possible for a great work to appear, he replied, No, it was not possible, it is not possible yet, it will become possible once it has appeared: 'If a man of talent or genius emerges, if he creates a work, then it is real and it thereby becomes retrospectively, retroactively possible.'[26]

Transposed to events, this means that they first take place, ex nihilo as it were, as something unpredictable. Only then can they be conceived as possible. This is the temporal paradox, the reversed temporality that designates the event as such.

As a general rule, we conceive of an ascending line running from the impossible to the possible, then to the real. Now, what marks out the true event is precisely that the real and the possible come into being simultaneously and are immediately imagined. But this relates to living events, to a living temporality, to a depth of time that no longer exists at all in real time.

Real time is violence done to time, violence done to the event. With the instantaneity of the Virtual and the precession of models, it is the whole depth of field of the durée, of origin and end, that is taken from us. It is the loss of an ever-deferred time and its replacement by an immediate, definitive time.

26. Henri Bergson, La pensée et le mouvant. Third edition (Paris: PUF, 1990), p. 110.

Things have only to be concentrated into an immediate present-ness by accentuating the simultaneity of all networks and all points on the globe for time to be reduced to its smallest simple element, the instant – which is no longer even a 'present' moment, but embodies the absolute reality of time in a total abstraction, thus prevailing against the irruption of any event and the eventuality of death.

Such is 'real time', the time of communication, information and perpetual interaction: the finest deterrence-space of time and events. On the real-time screen, by way of simple digital manipulation, all possibilities are potentially realized – which puts an end to their possibility. Through electronics and cybernetics, all desires, all play of identity and all interactive potentialities are programmed in and auto-programmed. The fact that everything here is realized from the outset prevents the emergence of any singular event.

Such is the violence of real time, which is also the violence of information.

Real time dematerializes both the future dimension and the past; it dematerializes historical time, pulverizes the real event. The Shoah, the year 2000 – it did not take place, it will not take place.

It even pulverizes the present event in news coverage [*l'information*], which is merely its instantaneous image-feedback.

News coverage is coupled with the illusion of present time, of presence – this is the media illusion of the world 'live' and, at the same time, the horizon of disappearance of the real event.

Hence the dilemma posed by all the images we receive: uncertainty regarding the truth of the event as soon as the news media are involved.

As soon as they are both involved in and involved by the course of phenomena, it is the news media that are the event. It is the event of news coverage that substitutes itself for coverage of the event.

The historic time of the event, the psychological time of affects, the subjective time of judgement and will, the objective time of reality – these are all simultaneously thrown into question by real time.

If there were a subject of history, a subject of knowledge, a subject of power, these have all disappeared in the obliteration by real time of distance, of the pathos of distance, in the integral realization of the world by information.

Before the event it is too early for the possible.
After the event it is too late for the possible.

It is too late also for representation, and nothing will really be able to account for it. September 11th, for example, is there first – only then do its possibility and its causes catch up with it, through all the discourses that will attempt to explain it. But it is as impossible to represent that event as it was to forecast it before it occurred. The CIA's experts had at their disposal all the information on the possibility of an attack, but they simply didn't believe in it. It was beyond imagining. Such an event always is. It is beyond all possible causes (and perhaps even, as Italo Svevo suggests, causes are merely a misunderstanding that prevents the world from being what it is).

We have, then, to pass through the non-event of news coverage (information) to detect what resists that coverage. To find, as it were, the 'living coin' of the event. To make a literal analysis of it, against all the machinery of commentary and stage-management that merely neutralizes it.

Only events set free from news and information (and us with them) create a fantastic longing. These alone are 'real', since there is nothing to explain them and the imagination welcomes them with open arms.

There is in us an immense desire for events.

And an immense disappointment, as all the contents of the information media are desperately inferior to the power of the broadcasting machinery. This disproportionality creates a demand that is ready to swoop on any incident, to crystallize on any catastrophe. And the pathetic contagion that sweeps through crowds on some particular occasion (the death of Diana, the World Cup) has no other cause. It isn't a question of voyeurism or letting off steam. It's a spontaneous reaction to an immoral situation: the excess of information creates an immoral situation, in that it has no equivalent in the real event. Automatically, one wants a maximal event, a 'fateful' event – which repairs this immense banalization of life by the information machine. We dream of senseless events that will free us from this tyranny of meaning and the constraint of causes.

We live in terror both of the excess of meaning and of total meaninglessness.

And in the banal context of social and personal life these excessive events are the equivalent of the excess of signifier in language for Lévi-Strauss: namely, that which founds it as symbolic function.

Desire for events, desire for non-events – the two drives are simultaneous and, doubtless, each as powerful as the other.

Hence this mix of jubilation and terror, of secret elation and remorse. Elation linked not so much to death as to the unpredictable, to which we are so partial.

All the justifications merely mask precisely this obscure desire for events, for overthrowing the order of things, whatever it may be.

A perfectly sacrilegious desire for the irruption of evil, for the restitution of a secret rule, which, in the form of a totally unjustified event (natural catastrophes are similarly unjustified), re-establishes something like a balance between the forces of good and evil.

Our moral protestations are directly proportionate to the immoral fascination that the automatic reversibility of evil exerts on us.

They say Diana was a victim of the 'society of the spectacle' and that we were passive voyeurs of her death. But there was a much more complex dramaturgy going on, a collective scenario in which Diana herself was not innocent (in terms of display of self), but in which the masses played an immediate role in a positive 'reality show' of the public and private life of Lady Di with the media as interface. The paparazzi were merely the vehicles, together with the media, of this lethal interaction, and behind them all of us, whose desire shapes the media – we who are the mass and the medium, the network and the electric current.

There are no actors or spectators any more. We are all immersed in the same reality, in the same revolving responsibility, in a single destiny that is merely the fulfilment of a collective desire. Here again we are not far removed from Stockholm Syndrome: we are the hostages of news coverage, but we acquiesce secretly in this hostage-taking.

At the same time we violently desire events, any event, provided it is exceptional. And we also desire just as passionately that nothing should happen, that things should be in order and remain so, even at the cost of a disaffection with existence that is itself unbearable. Hence the sudden convulsions and the contradictory affects that ensue from them: jubilation or terror.

Hence also two types of analysis: the one that responds to the extreme singularity of the event and the other whose function might be said to be to routinize it – an orthodox thinking and a paradoxical thinking. Between the two there is no longer room for merely critical thought.

Like it or not, the situation has become radicalized. And if we think this radicalization is that of evil – evil being ultimately the disappearance of all mediation, leaving only the clash between extremes – then we must acknowledge this situation and confront the problem of evil.

We do not have to plump for the one or the other.

We experience the simultaneous attraction and repulsion of the event and the non-event. Just as, according to Hannah Arendt, we are confronted in any action with the unforeseeable and the irreversible.

But, since the irreversible today is the movement towards virtual ascendancy over the world, towards total control and technological 'enframing', towards the tyranny of absolute prevention and technical security, we have left to us only the unpredictable, the luck of the event.

And just as Mallarmé said that a throw of the dice would never abolish chance – that is to say, there would never be an ultimate dice throw which, by its automatic perfection, would put an end to chance – so we may hope that virtual programming will never abolish events.

Never will the point of technical perfection and absolute prevention be reached where the fateful event can be said to have disappeared.

There will always be a chance for the troubling strangeness [*das Unheimliche*] of the event, as against the troubling monotony of the global order.

A fine metaphor for this is that video artist who had his camera trained on the Manhattan peninsula throughout the month of September 2001, in order to record the fact that nothing happens, in order to film the non-event.

And banality went right ahead and blew up in his camera lens with the Twin Towers!

Evil and Misfortune

Of evil in the pure state it is impossible to speak.

What one can speak of is the distinction between evil and misfortune, the reduction of evil to misfortune, and a culture of misfortune that is complicit with the hegemonic culture of happiness.[27]

The ideal opposition between good and evil has been reduced to the ideological opposition between happiness and misfortune. The reduction of good to happiness is as baneful as that of evil to misfortune, but this latter is more interesting because it shows up our humanistic vision more distinctly, that vision which sees man as naturally good, and evil and misfortune as mere accidents.

It is here, in the idea that man is good, or at least culturally perfectible, that we encounter our deepest imaginary conception, and with it our most serious confusion. For if misfortune is an accident and, ultimately, like sickness and poverty, a reparable accident (from the technical standpoint of integral happiness even death is no longer irreparable), evil, for its part, is not an accident. If misfortune is accidental, evil is *fatal*.[28] It is an original power and, in no sense, a dysfunction, vestige or mere obstacle standing in the way of good.

---

27. The key terms here are more evidently related at the lexical level in French: le Mal (evil), le malheur (misfortune), le bonheur (happiness).
28. Primarily in the sense of destined, fated to occur.

The sovereign hypothesis, the hypothesis of evil, is that man is not good by nature, not because he might be said to be bad, but because he is perfect as he is.

He is perfect in the sense that the fruit is perfect, but not more perfect than the flower, which is perfect in itself and is not the unfinished phase of a definitive state.

Nothing is definitive – or rather everything is. Every stage of evolution, every age of life, every moment of life, every animal or plant species, is perfect in itself. Every character, in its singular imperfection, in its matchless finitude, is incomparable.

This is what evolutionary thought tends to suppress in the name of a finality that can only be that of Good, to the – perfectly immoral – advantage of some particular species, for it is in evolutionism, in the idea of a progressive succession, that all discriminations are rooted.

If one takes each term in its singularity – and not in its particularity, referred to the universal – then each term is perfect; it is itself its own end.

In this way every detail of the world is perfect if it is not referred to some larger set.

In this way everything is perfect if it is not referred to its idea.

In this way the nothing is perfect since it is set against nothing.

And in this way evil is perfect when left to itself, to its own evil genius.

Such is man before being plunged into the idea of progress and into the technical imagining of happiness: he is both evil and perfection – like the Cathars, who, while recognizing the singular power of evil and its total hold over creation, called themselves perfect: the 'Perfecti'.

Ceronetti, in *L'occhiale malinconico,* writes: 'I find the philosophical idea of the fundamental misfortune of the human race quite alien. In Leopardi, the inalterable innocence of the victim is always presupposed and nature then strikes them down as though with some malignant tumour. ... I do not see innocence anywhere. I know men are base by nature and not by accident, but when I think "human condition", I lose any notion of happiness or misfortune – the night carries it away, all that remains is a hopeless puzzle.'

Or, again: 'I feel misfortune as a marginal burning sensation, which does not correspond to a vision of evil, of which it might be said merely to be an accident, a belated event.'

At bottom, the dogma of misfortune is too clear and too verifiable an idea to be fundamental. Evil is a confused, impenetrable idea. It is enigmatic in its very essence. Now, a tiny confused idea is always greater than a very big idea that is absolutely clear.

The idea of misfortune is, then, an easy solution.

Just as the idea of freedom is the easiest solution to the impossibility of thinking destiny and predestination, just as the idea of reality is the easiest solution to the impossibility of thinking the radical illusoriness of the world, so the idea of misfortune is the easiest solution to the impossibility of thinking evil.

This impossibility of thinking evil is matched only by the impossibility of imagining death.

Hence the question how an entire people was able to follow the Nazis in their enterprise of extermination is one that remains hopelessly insoluble for a rational thought, an Enlightenment thought that is incapable of thinking beyond an ideal version of man, incapable even of envisaging the absence of a response to such a question.

Unintelligence of evil, absence of insight into things by evil and therefore always the same discourse on the 'foul beast' and the same naïveté in the analysis of present events.

Our whole system of values excludes this predestination of evil.

Yet all it has invented, at the end of its burdensome therapy on the human species, is another way of making it disappear, that is to say, of ironically carrying the possibility of happiness to its opposite term, that of the perfect crime, that of integral misfortune, which was somehow waiting for it just at the end.

For you cannot liberate good without liberating evil, and that liberation is even more rapid than the liberation of good.

It is, in fact, no longer exactly a struggle between good and evil. It's a question of transparency.

Good is transparent: you can see through it.

Evil, by contrast, shows through: it is what you see when you see through.

Or alternatively, evil is the first hypothesis, the first supposition. Good is merely a transposition and a substitute product: the hypostasis of evil.

Good definitively scattered among the figures of evil. Anamorphosis of good.

Evil definitively scattered among the figures of good. Anamorphosis of evil.

It is only through the distorted, disseminated figures of evil that one can reconstitute, in perspective, the figure of good. It is only through the dispersed and falsely symmetrical figures of good that one can reconstitute the paradoxical figure of evil.

As it is only through the dispersion of the name of God in the labyrinth of the poem that you can sense the original figure running through it.

This way evil has of showing through in all the figures of good, this occult presence, is the matrix of all perverse effects and, singularly, of the fact that everything which stands opposed to the system today is merely an involuntary mirror to it.

So it is with all these developments in human rights, humanitarianism and all these things '*sans frontières*' that merely hasten the circulation of the New World Order for which they stand surety. Without that being anyone's strategy.

In this sense, the hypothesis of evil is never that of a determined ill-will, but the hypothesis of a rational concatenation, of normality on the move – a teleonomy that is particularly tangible in all the recent wars where the right of humanitarian intervention clearly takes over the role of extending that New Order. The Kosovans were not just human shields for the Serbs; the whole refugee drama served as a humanitarian shield for the West.

An entirely synchronous disconnect: the refugee drama was treated as a 'humanitarian' catastrophe, while the 'surgical' air strikes were unfolding just as implacably. Thus the apotropaic figures of good ensure the continuation of evil, just as (in Macedonio Fernández's writings) the vicissitudes of meaning and value keep the Nothing in being.

As Ceronetti says, 'Concrete salvation takes the form of an accelerated destruction.' But, in a way, it is not evil, but good that is manifestly at the controls of the suicide locomotive.

Thinking based on evil is not pessimistic; it is the thinking based on misfortune that is pessimistic because it wants desperately to escape evil or, alternatively, to revel in it.

Thought, for its part, does not cure human misfortune, the terrible obviousness of which it absorbs for purposes of some unknown transformation. Pessimism excludes any depth that eludes its negative judgement, whereas thought wishes to penetrate magically beyond the fracture of the visible. The rays of the black sun of pessimism do not reach down to the floor of the abyss.

Absolute depth knows neither good nor evil.

Thus the intelligence of evil goes far beyond pessimism.

In reality, the only genuinely pessimistic, nihilistic vision is that of good since, at bottom, from the humanist point of view, the whole of history is nothing but crime. Cain killing Abel is already a crime against humanity (there were only two of them!) and isn't original sin already a crime against humanity too? This is all absurd, and, from the standpoint of good, the effort to rehabilitate the world's violence is a hopeless exercise. All the more so as, without all these crimes, there simply wouldn't be any history.

'If the evil in man were eliminated,' says Montaigne, 'you would destroy the fundamental conditions of life.'

Everything comes from this confusion between evil and misfortune.

Evil is the world as it is and as it has been, and we can take a lucid view of this. Misfortune is the world as it ought never to have been – but in the name of what? In the name of what ought to be, in the name of God or a transcendent ideal, of a good it would be very hard to define.

We may take a criminal view of crime: that is tragedy. Or we may take a recriminative view of it: that is humanitarianism; it is the pathetic, sentimental vision, the vision that calls constantly for reparation.

We have here all the *Ressentiment* that comes from the depths of a genealogy of morals and calls within us for reparation of our own lives.

This retrospective compassion, this conversion of evil into misfortune, is the twentieth century's finest industry.

First as a mental blackmailing operation, to which we are all victim, even in our actions, from which we may hope only for a lesser evil – keep a low profile, decriminalize your existence! – then as source of a tidy profit, since misfortune (in all its forms, from suffering to insecurity, from oppression to depression) represents a symbolic capital, the exploitation of which, even more than the exploitation of happiness, is endlessly profitable: it is a goldmine with a seam running through each of us.

Contrary to received opinion, misfortune is easier to manage than happiness – that is why it is the ideal solution to the problem of evil. It is misfortune that is most distinctly opposed to evil and to the principle of evil, of which it is the denial.

Just as freedom ends in total liberation and, in abreaction to that liberation, in new servitudes, so the ideal of happiness leads to a whole culture of misfortune, of recrimination, repentance, compassion and victimhood.

We go on discarding elements of freedom in all kinds of ways, while continuing to speak up for it.

We go on dreaming of perfect happiness, while sensing the potential boredom of paradise. For we know what Hell is like and those burning in Hell, since Hell is never being able to do anything but evil. But how is it with those in Paradise who will no longer have any idea of evil? God alone knows what awaits them.

It is here and now, however, that we are confronted with the tedium of the artificial paradises, with ideal living conditions. And it is by hypersensitivity to these ideal conditions that we abreact and tend towards misfortune as the most sustainable solution – a kind of escape route from the terroristic happiness plot. The despair of having everything.[29]

29. This sentence in English in the original.

Yet we do not, for all that, move closer to evil or to the essence of evil. On the contrary, we move further away from it, for the closer you get to the comfortable obviousness of misfortune, the further you move from the invisible continuity of evil.

'*Bis Gottes Fehle hilft,*' says Hölderlin. 'Until God's absence comes to our aid.'

The death of God is, in fact, the deliverance from all responsibility to another world. But our responsibility for this world then becomes total, and there is no longer any possible redemption.

Or, rather, redemption changes meaning: it is no longer the redemption of man and his sin, but the redemption of the death of God. That death has to be redeemed by a compulsive effort to transform the world. One has to ensure one's salvation at all costs by realizing the world for better or for worse.

A performance that tops off the one described by Max Weber in *The Spirit of Capitalism*: that of transforming the world into wealth for the greater glory of God. But it is no longer a question now of his glory; it is a question of his death and of exorcizing it. The point is to make the world transparent and operational by extirpating from it any illusion and any evil force.

And so, under the hegemony of good, everything is getting better and, at the same time, going from bad to worse: no hell any more, and no damnation. Everything becomes susceptible of redemption. From this point on, good and evil, which were still opposing powers, but linked to each other in transcendence, are to be dissociated for the purposes of a definitive realization of the world under the banner of happiness.

In fact, this idea of happiness bears merely a distant relation to good. For if good is moral in essence, happiness – the performance of happiness – is in essence perfectly immoral.

It is to such an evangelization that we can ascribe all the manifest signs of well-being and accomplishment offered to us by a paradisiac civilization subject to the eleventh commandment, the commandment that sweeps away all others: 'Be happy and show all the signs of happiness!'

We can see this demand for universal redemption in the way all current violence and injustice is being put on trial, and also, retrospectively, all the crimes and violent events of the past: the French Revolution, slavery, original sin and battered wives, the ozone layer and sexual harassment. In short, the investigative process for the Last Judgement is already well under way and we are doomed first to condemn, then to absolve and whitewash the whole of our history; to exterminate evil from even the tiniest interstices, so as to offer the image of a radiant universe ready to pass over into the next world.

An inhuman, superhuman, all-too-human undertaking?

And why fuel this eternal repentance, this chain reaction of bad conscience?

Because everything must be saved.

This is where we have got to today. Everything will be redeemed, the whole past will be rehabilitated, buffed up to the point of transparency. As for the future, it is better and worse yet: everything will be genetically modified to attain the biological and democratic perfection of the species.

The salvation that was defined by the equivalence of merit and grace will be defined, once the fixation with evil and Hell has been overcome, by the equivalence of genes and performance.

147

To tell the truth, once happiness becomes the general equivalent of salvation, pure and simple, then heaven itself is no longer needed. From the point when everyone is potentially saved, no one is. Salvation no longer has any meaning.

This is the destiny that beckons for our democratic enterprise: it is stifled at birth for having forgotten the necessary discrimination, for the omission of evil.

We need, then, an irrevocable presence of evil, an evil from which there is no possible redemption, an irrevocable discrimination, a perpetual duality of Heaven and Hell, and even, in a sense, a predestination of evil, for there can be no destiny without some predestination.

There is nothing immoral in this. According to the rules of the game, there is nothing immoral in some losing and others winning, or even in everyone losing. What would be immoral would be for everyone to win. This is the contemporary ideal of our democracy: that all should be saved. But that is possible only at the cost of a perpetual inflation and upping of the stakes.

And this is reassuring, since the imperative of salvation, of the individual state of grace, will always be thwarted by some challenge or passion from elsewhere, and any form of personal beatitude may be sacrificed to something more vital, which may be of the order of the will in Schopenhauer's terms or of the will to power in Nietzsche's, but which, in any event, retains the fateful quality of that which, in opposition to any happy finality, is predestined to come to pass.

Behind its euphoric exaltation, this imperative of maximum performance bears within it evil and misfortune in the form of a deep disavowal and a secret disillusionment.

Perhaps performance is merely a collective form of human sacrifice, but disembodied and distilled into our entire technological machinery.

In this strange world, where everything is potentially available – the body, sex, space, money, pleasure – to be taken or rejected *en bloc*, everything is there; nothing has disappeared physically, but everything has disappeared metaphysically. 'As if by magic,' one might say, except that it has disappeared not so much by enchantment as by disenchantment.

Individuals, such as they are, become exactly what they are. Without transcendence and without image, they carry on their lives like a useless function in the eyes of another world, irrelevant even in their own eyes.

And they do what they do all the better for the fact that there is no other possibility. No authority to appeal to.

They have sacrificed their lives to their functional existences. They are one with the exact numerical calculation of their lives and their performance.

Summoned to get the greatest efficiency and pleasure out of themselves, human beings are suddenly at odds and their existences dislocated.

An existence realized, then, but at the same time denied, thwarted, disowned.

Wherever humans are condemned to total freedom or to an ideal fulfilment, this automatic abreaction to their own good and their own happiness seeps in.

This imperative of maximum performance also comes into contradiction with the moral law, which dictates that everyone shall be put on an equal basis and everything set to zero in the name of democracy and an equal division of opportunity and advantage. From the perspective of universal redemption no one must stand out.

For justice to be done, all privilege must disappear; everyone is called on to shed any specific qualities and to become once again an elementary particle – collective happiness being that of the lowest common denominator. This is like potlatch in reverse, each outbidding the other in insignificance, while zealously cultivating their tiniest difference and cobbling together their multiple identities.

Recrimination means going back over the crime to correct its trajectory and its effects. This is what we are doing in going back over the whole of our history, over the criminal history of the human species, so that we may do penance right now as we await the Last Judgement.

Hence the immense syndrome of repentance and rewriting (historical rewriting for now, but with the genetic, biological rewriting of the species yet to come) that has taken hold of this *fin de siècle*, from the perspective still of deserving salvation and of offering the image of an ideal victim at the last.

A 'clean-up' of all the violent events of past centuries, in order to bring them under the new jurisdiction of human rights and crimes against humanity. The latest episode of this revisionist madness is the proposal that slavery and the slave trade be condemned as a crime against humanity.

The rectification of the past in terms of our new human-itarian awareness. Or, in other words, in the purest colonial tradition, the imperialism of repentance! The idea is to allow the 'populations concerned' to carry out their mourning and draw a line under this page of their history in order to enter fully upon the path of modern history. Perhaps the Africans will even be able to turn this moral acknowledgement into damage claims on the same terms that have been granted to survivors of the Shoah.

Then we shall see no end to compensating, redeeming and rehabilitating, and all we shall have done will have been to add to the traditional exploitation the hypocritical absolution of all violence.

A victim economy, a political economy of misfortune: a positive tradeable stock, which, in all its forms, has substituted itself for the impossible exchange of evil.

A differential of victimhood that nowhere pays off so well, is nowhere so lucrative today, as in the negotiation of oneself as waste (something magnificently illustrated by contemporary art).

An inexhaustible seam, since this negative affect is the most widely distributed of all. We can always count on this denial of self that smoulders within each of us, much more than on pride, self-regard or self-love. Much more even than on pleasure or the taste for pleasure, we can count on this wallowing in misfortune.

Many people's only talent in life is to mobilize this affect and this alternative solution. 'After hatred, the fundamental enemy of the human race is remorse,' says Spinoza. But hatred and remorse are one and the same: it is remorse at individuation and at the breaking of the symbolic pact that engenders self-hatred and *Ressentiment*.

Rendered official in this way, self-criticism and repentance have even become a mode of government: politicians constantly offer up the mirror of their uselessness for the assent of their fellow citizens, who can thus continue to live in contempt for themselves through the contempt they feel for their political class. For, if the love of others is the path taken by one's own self-love – La Rochefoucauld virtually made a set of rules out of this – one may also detest oneself through the hatred and contempt one feels for others.

Everyone counts on deriving the secondary gains from this vicious circle and misfortune is exchanged on the Stock Exchange of Values, whereas evil is inconvertible.

Immediate conversion, in the name of the law, of misfortune into earnings – the pay-off for an accident or for depression, the commercial equivalent of any setback, any handicap: rape, sexual harassment, even birth itself, regarded as a congenital affliction (for example, the blind, deaf, mute and mentally retarded child who was recently granted life-long compensation for the fact of being born).

Today this chronicle of recrimination and compensation covers the entire 'social' field, which is now merged with the fields of insurance and security.

And this model of repentance and reparation of all wrongs has been shifted on to a quite other level: the genetic reparation of all the deficits of the human species.

All this shows a very mediocre idea of oneself – always imputing misfortune to some objective cause.

Once it has been exorcized by causes, misfortune is no longer a problem: it becomes susceptible of a causal solution and, above all, it originates elsewhere – in original sin, in history, in the social order, or in natural perversion. In short, it originates in an objectivity into which we exile it the better to be rid of it. Once again, this bespeaks very little pride and self-respect.

In the past, what struck you down was your destiny, your personal *fatum*. You didn't look for some 'objective' cause of this or some attenuating circumstance, which would amount to saying we have no part in what happens to us. There is something humiliating in that.

The intelligence of evil begins with the hypothesis that our ills come to us from an evil genius that is our own.

Let us be worthy of our 'perversity', of our evil genius, let us measure up to our tragic involvement in what happens to us (including good fortune).

In a word, let us not be imbeciles, for imbecility in the literal sense lies in the superficial reference to misfortune and exemption from evil.

This is how we make imbeciles of the victims themselves, by confining them to their condition of victim. And by the compassion we show them we engage in a kind of false advertising for them.

We take no account of what degree of choice and defiance, of connivence with oneself, of – unconscious or quasi-deliberate – provocative relation to evil there may be in AIDS, in drug-taking, in suffering and alienation, in voluntary servitude – in this acting-out in the fatal zone.

It is the same with suicide, which is always ascribed to depressive motivations with no account taken of an originality of, an original will to commit, the act itself (Canetti speaks in the same way of the interpretation of dreams as a violence done to dreams that takes no account of their literalness).

So, the understanding of misfortune is everywhere substituted for the intelligence of evil. Now, unlike the former, this latter rests on the rejection of the presumption of innocence. By contrast with that understanding, we are all presumptive wrongdoers – but not responsible ones, for, in the last instance, we do not have to answer for ourselves – that is the business of destiny or of the divinity.

For the act we commit, it is right we should be dealt with – and indeed punished – accordingly. We are never innocent of that act in the sense of having nothing to do with it or being victims of it. But this does not mean we are answerable for it either, as that would suppose we were answerable for ourselves, that we were invested with total power over ourselves, which is a subjective illusion.

It's a good thing we don't possess that power or that respons-ibility. A good thing we are not the causes of ourselves – that at least confers some degree of innocence on us. For the rest, we are forever complicit in what we do, even if we are not answerable to anyone.

So we are both irresponsible and without excuses.

Never explain, never complain.[30]

One must never confess to being unfortunate or claim to be unfortunate, and hence in some way innocent and a victim.

There is no presumption of innocence and it is better to be part of evil than party to misfortune.

So, to say of a woman she is an innocent victim of seduction, that she has no part in the fact of being seduced, is an offence to femininity itself.

In this way, beyond good and evil, that dual relation is played out in which the victim ceases to be a victim by an active complicity with his/her own misfortune.

The extreme case of Stockholm Syndrome is like this, where the hostage ends up going over to the hostage-taker's cause – an incomprehensible turn of events if one cannot conceive that this complicity of the victim equates to a symbolic transference and forms part of the ironic essence of evil.

Which means there is nowhere a definition of Good or for anyone a clear definition of happiness – and that nothing is for the best in the best of all worlds.

The paradox may extend as far as the moral obligation of gratitude to the other for the evil he has done you, as illustrated by the following Japanese story, which is sublime, but difficult for our Western morality to accept, in which a

30. This phrase in English in the original.

woman decides not to save the life of a drowning child since, she says, 'You would owe me such a debt of gratitude that your entire life would not suffice to pay it back.'

Is there not also the profoundest pleasure in bitterness? No satisfaction, no victory, will ever be the equivalent of the bitter plenitude of the sense of injustice. It revels in itself. It draws on the very roots of an inner revenge on existence. Who, in the light of that, could claim to give a definition of happiness?

Complex as is this entanglement of good and evil, so too is it difficult to pass beyond good and evil when the very distinction between the two has disappeared.

One may reject all this.

The fact remains that the hypothesis of evil, of the lack of distinction between good and evil and our deep complicity with the worst, is always present, rendering all our actions impenetrable. But it is itself a principle of action and doubtless one of the most powerful.

I am playing devil's advocate here.

But if you reject this hypothesis you can always think in terms of a wager of the Pascalian type. What Pascal says, more or less, is this: you can always content yourself with a secular existence and its advantages, but it's much more fun with the hypothesis of God. With just a few sacrifices to make in exchange for eternal salvation, the advantages are much greater.

Where we are concerned, this same wager becomes: you can always get by with the hypothesis of good and happiness, but it's much more fun with the hypothesis of evil.

A variant of the same wager would be: you can always get by with the hypothesis of reality, but it's much more fun with the hypothesis of radical illusion.

We should transfer on to reality – or rather on to the non-existence of reality – Pascal's wager on the existence of God.

Pascal: It's to your advantage to believe in the existence of God and eternal life since, if they don't exist, you won't have lost much by sacrificing your life. On the other hand, if they do exist, you stand to gain infinitely.

Reality: It's to your advantage not to believe in it, since if you believe in it and it doesn't exist, you're duped and swindled and you will die stupid.

If you don't believe in it and it doesn't exist, you win on all counts.

If you don't believe in it and it does exist, you retain the benefit of the doubt, since there will never be any conclusive proof of its existence, any more than of the existence of God (moreover, if it exists, given what it is, it is better to be parted from it as quickly as possible).

Clearly this is the opposite choice to that of Pascal, who opts for God. But it is the same wager. And, in any event, no one is forced to gamble.

It is all down to the fact that the Devil had an unhappy childhood and one cannot accuse him of maleficence when he is merely doing the dirty work, in accordance with the providential designs of which he is merely the instrument. This poor devil, Mephisto, who always desires evil and always does good, really has no need of an advocate.

It would seem rather to be God who needed one. He who created the world and, as a result, took upon himself an infinite debt, and who has been constantly passing that debt on to mankind, the entire history of which since then is one of wrongdoing.

And worse: to that enforced guilt he added humiliation.

For mankind is faced with the impossibility of making a sacrifice to equal this gift of God's, the impossibility of making restitution and wiping away the debt. Being unable to take up this challenge, it has to humble itself and give thanks. It is at this point that God chose to cancel the debt himself by sending his beloved son to sacrifice himself on the cross. He pretends to humble himself, and, in so doing, inflicts an even greater humiliation on humanity by making it conscious of its impotence. Henceforth humanity is condemned to give thanks, not just for having been created, but for having been saved (very relatively, as it happens, for this humiliation does not mean it will be spared the Last Judgement).

This is the greatest act of manipulation ever.

And it succeeded far beyond its objective – even beyond the death of God, since we have taken it over today, augmented by the guilt of that death (God's cunning is infinite).

We mimic here below this humiliation received from God: in victimhood, humanitarianism, self-derision and self-deprecation, in this immense sacrificial effort that stands in, in our case, for redemption.

We could have taken advantage of the death of God to be free of the debt. But we didn't take that option. We chose rather to deepen the debt, to eternalize it in an endless performance, a sacrificial accumulation, as though we had already internalized God's judgement.

'God's absence' has not come to our aid – contrary to Hölderlin's expectation (*'Bis Gottes Fehle hilft'*).

In fact God himself is complicit in all this.

God himself is in league with the principle of evil.

We have this from the fabulous tale of Lilith and Saekina which the Kabbalah recounts (Primo Levi).

When Lilith, the first woman created by God as the equal of Adam, had rebelled, God chose to create Eve, the fruit of

Adam's rib, since the first man clearly needed a companion. However, God realized at this point that it is not good to be alone and he chose a wife for himself, Saekina, who was none other than his own presence in the world (fantastic: he marries his own presence in the world!). Saekina eventually takes umbrage at God's behaviour toward the Jews (when the temple at Jerusalem is destroyed – why did he not protect them better?). She runs off, going out into the world to do Good. And what does God do then? He takes a mistress. And who is this mistress? It is Lilith, who is none other than the principle of evil, a rebel against God and an unbeliever.

So God cheats on his own presence in the world with the – feminine – principle of evil! He betrays the integrality, the completeness, of the world – his union with Saekina – for an (adulterous) union with duality, which he takes as his mistress.

Now, that mistress, Lilith, has not, like Eve, issued from Adam as a kind of by-product. She exists *principio suo*, entirely autonomously, which makes her the emblem of evil... Well, God makes a pact with all that. He plots against his own presence and against the reproduction of the species by allying unnaturally with the emblem of evil.

And thus, while Saekina, the wife, continues to do Good throughout the world, she, Lilith, continues to do evil with God's connivance.

And so long as she is there, says the Kabbalah, everything will go from bad to worse.

The Intelligence of Evil

This, then, is the way we must begin, with the secret intelligence of – the secret insight into – duality and reversibility, with speaking evil as in a mental Theatre of Cruelty.

Above all, we must not confuse the idea of evil with some kind of objective existence of evil. That has no more meaning than an objective existence of the Real; it is merely the moral and metaphysical illusion of Manichaeism that it is possible to will evil, to do evil, or, alternatively, to denounce it and combat it.

Evil has no objective reality.

Quite the contrary, it consists in the diverting of things from their 'objective' existence, in their reversal, their 'return' (I wonder if we might not even interpret Nietzsche's 'Eternal Return' in this sense – not as an endless cycle, not as a repetition, but as a turning about, as a reversible form of becoming – *die ewige Umkehr*).

In this sense, in precisely the same way as Canetti conceives vengeance, evil too is automatic.

You cannot will it. That is an illusion and a misconception. The evil you can will, the evil you can do and which, most of the time, merges with violence, suffering and death, has nothing to do with this reversible form of evil. We might even say that those who deliberately practise evil certainly have no insight into it, since their act supposes the intentionality of a subject, whereas this reversibility of evil is the reversibility of a form.

And it is, at bottom, the form itself that is intelligent, insightful: with evil it is not a question of an object to be understood; we are dealing with a form that understands us.

In the 'intelligence of evil' we have to understand that it is evil that is intelligent, that it is it which thinks us – in the sense that it is implied automatically in every one of our acts.

For it is not possible for any act whatever or any kind of talk not to have two sides to it; not to have a reverse side, and hence a dual existence. And this contrary to any finality or objective determination.

This dual form is irreducible, indissociable from all existence. It is therefore pointless to wish to localize it and even more so to wish to denounce it. The denunciation of evil is still of the order of morality, of a moral evaluation.

Now, evil is immoral, not in the way a crime is immoral, but in the way a form is. And the intelligence of evil itself is immoral – it does not aspire to any value judgement, it does not do evil, it speaks it.

The idea of evil as a malign force, a maleficent agency, a deliberate perversion of the order of the world, is a deep-rooted superstition.

It is echoed at the world level in the phantasmic projection of the Axis of Evil, and in the Manichaean struggle against that power.

This is all part of the same imaginary.

Hence the principle of the prevention, the forestalling, the prophylaxis, of evil; rather than morality or metaphysics, what we have today is an infection, a microbial epidemic, the corruption of a world whose predestined end is presumed to lie in good.

A more subtle misconception is that of a hypostasis of evil as indestructible reality, a kind of primal scene, a sort of substratum of accumulated death-drive.

The radicality of evil is seen as that of a naturally inevitable force, associated always with violence, suffering and death.

Hence Sloterdijk's hypothesis that 'the reality of reality is the eternal return of violence'. To which he opposes a 'pacifism that is in keeping with our most advanced theoretical intuitions, a deep-level pacifism, based on a radical analysis of the circularity of violence, deciphering the forces that determine its eternal return'.

A radical analysis, then, to remedy the radical evil.

But can a 'radical' analysis have a finality of whatever kind?

Is it not itself part of the process of evil?

However that may be, duality and evil are not the same as violence.

The dual form, the *agon*, is a symbolic form and, as such, it might be said to be much nearer to seduction and challenge than to violence. Closer to metamorphosis and becoming than to force and violence.

If there were a force of evil, a reality of evil, a source and an origin of evil, one could confront it strategically with all the forces of good.

But if evil is a form, and most of the time a form that is deeply buried, one can only bring out that form and come to an understanding with it [*être en intelligence avec elle*].

This is how it is, for example, with the Theatre of Cruelty: in that gestural and scenic externalization of all the 'perverse' possibilities of the human spirit, within the framework of an exploration of the roots of evil, there is never any question of tragic catharsis. The point, rather, is to play out fully these perverse possibilities and make drama out of them, but without sublimating or resolving them.

'To speak evil' is to speak this fateful, paradoxical situation that is the reversible concatenation of good and evil.

That is to say that the irresistible pursuit of good, the movement of Integral Reality – for this is what good is: it is the movement towards integrality, towards an integral order of the world – is immoral. The eschatological perspective of a better world is in itself immoral. For the reason that our technical mastery of the world, our technical approach to good, having become an automatic and irresistible mechanism, none of this is any longer of the order of morality or of any kind of finality.

Nor is to speak and read evil the same thing as vulgar nihilism, the nihilism of a denunciation of all values, that of the prophets of doom.

To denounce the reality contract or the reality 'conspiracy' is not at all nihilistic. It is not in any sense to deny an obvious fact, in the style of 'All is sign, nothing is real – nothing is true, everything is simulacrum' – an absurd proposition since it is also a realist one!

It is one thing to note the vanishing of the real into the Virtual, another to deny it so as to pass beyond the real and the Virtual.

It is one thing to reject morality in the name of a vulgar immoralism, another to do so, like Nietzsche so as to pass beyond good and evil.

To be 'nihilistic' is to deny things at their greatest degree of intensity, not in their lowest versions. Now, existence and self-evidence have always been the lowest forms.

If there is nihilism, then, it is not a nihilism of value, but a nihilism of form. It is to speak the world in its radicality, in its dual, reversible form, and this has never meant banking on catastrophe, any more than on violence.

No finality, either positive or negative, is ever the last word in the story.

And the Apocalypse itself is a facile solution.

To speak evil is to say that in every process of domination and conflict is forged a secret complicity, and in every process of consensus and balance, a secret antagonism.

'Voluntary servitude' and the 'involuntary', suicidal failing of the power systems – two phenomena that are every bit as strange as each other, on the fringes of which we can make out all the ambivalence of political forms. This is to say that:

– immigration, the social question of immigration in our societies, is merely the most visible and crudest illustration of the internal exile of the European in his own society.

– terrorism can be interpreted as the expression of the internal dislocation of a power that has become all-powerful – a global violence immanent in the world-system itself. Hence the attempt to extirpate it as an objective evil is delusional given that, in its very absurdity, it is the expression of the condemnation that power pronounces on itself.

That, as Brecht said of fascism (that it was made up of both fascism and antifascism), terrorism is made up of terrorism and anti-terrorism together.

And that, if it is the incarnation of fanaticism and violence, it is the incarnation of the violence of those who denounce it at the same time as of their impotence, and of the absurdity of combating it frontally without having understood anything of this diabolical complicity and this reversibility of terror.

The violence you mete out is always the mirror of the violence you inflict on yourself. The violence you inflict on yourself is always the mirror of the violence you mete out.

This is the intelligence of evil.

If terrorism is evil – and it certainly is in its form, and not at all in the sense in which George W. Bush understands it – then it is this intelligence of Evil we need; the intelligence of, the insight into, this internal convulsion of the world order, of which terrorism is both the event-moment and the image-feedback.

For Whom Does the Knell of Politics Toll?

It is the secret failing of politics that it is no longer able to think evil.

Politics is the site of the exercise of evil, of the management of evil, scattered into individual souls and collective manifestations in all its forms – privilege, vice and corruption. It is the inescapable fate of power to take this accursed share upon itself, and that of men in power to be sacrificed to it, a privilege from which they expect to derive all the secondary gains.

But practising evil is difficult and one may suppose that they are constantly trying to pass the buck in every way possible.

In the past, power was arbitrary, which corresponded to the fact that it came from elsewhere, being devolved from on high without regard for inherent qualities – being, in a sense, predestined.

Royal power was like this. Hence Louis XVI's stupefaction on being told that the insurgents wanted power. How can you want power?

It is given to you, and all you can do is exercise it, like it or not. No one can rid you of it. The idea of deposing the King is as absurd as the idea of a constitutional God.

Power is an obligation and one must not demand it, one must consent to it.

On the other hand, it is arbitrary since, for that very reason, it does not have to justify itself. The only solution was, indeed, the death of the King, that is to say, the restoration of the accursed share to the whole of society.

That each should have his or her portion of the 'accursed share' is the democratic principle. But it seems the 'citizens' do not really want to submit to this sovereign obligation and they are afraid of their own arbitrary power.

It will, then, be devolved to a few – these will be the politicians, who themselves most often have only one idea: to give it away. You have only to see them redistributing power in every possible way – on the one hand, to prove to themselves that they have it, and, on the other, to ensure that no one escapes it, for those who refuse it are dangerous. 'If I knew,' said Canetti, 'that there still are on this earth *some human beings without any power* I would say that nothing is lost.'

The great danger for the very existence of politics is not that human beings should compete to take power, *but that they should not want it.*

Those in power have a twofold problem: in the political order, the problem of wielding power; and in the symbolic order, the problem of getting rid of it.

It's exactly the same as with money: the economic problem is to earn money and make it work for you; the symbolic problem is to be rid of it at all costs, to lift that curse from yourself. And it's an almost impossible task.

You have only to see those American start-up companies, suddenly made rich by speculation and desperately trying to hand out donations right and left, trying to invest in all kinds of charitable trusts and foundations for promoting the arts. Alas, by some fearful curse they just make even more profit. Money takes its revenge by multiplying.

It is the same with power: in spite of all the rituals of inter-action, participation and devolution, power is not soluble in exchange, and the dominated are too cunning really to take their part in it. They prefer to live in the shade of power.

So, when it comes to power or money, no absolution; the defiance remains total and the ordeal of the rich and powerful is, in this sense, inescapable. By their very privilege they are cast in the role of victims, since they are burdened with all the responsibility we have relinquished, a responsibility of which they are the stooges and mercenaries.

The 'social contract' ideally represented the portion of sov-ereignty citizens relinquished to the state, but nowadays we would be talking rather of *the relinquished, alienated part of themselves that they rid themselves of in order to retain their sovereignty.*

In the same way, more or less, as we once handed over the management of money to the Jews and the usurers, we have passed the dirty work of management and representation off to a body of people that has by that very act become accursed and untouchable, and which expects to take the profits from it in the form of 'power'.

When they describe themselves as servants of the people and the nation, they do not know how right they are. They are, in fact, the occupants of a servile – traditionally servile – function: the administration of things. May God protect and keep them!

This discredit resurfaces in the way the political class are per-petually on trial, in this endless question of lack of public confidence for which they can find no answer – a repudiation that sounds like an invitation to suicide, the only political act worthy of the name.

We dream of seeing the political class resigning *en masse* because we dream of seeing what a social body without a political superstructure would be like (as we dream of seeing what a world without representation would be like): a massive relief, a massive collective catharsis.

In every trial, in every public challenge to a politician or statesman, this millenarian demand (naturally always thwarted) resurfaces: the demand for a power that would speak out against itself, unmask itself, giving way to a radical, unhoped-for and, admittedly, hopeless situation, but one from which the inextricable tangle of mental corruption would be removed.

However, this art of disappearing, this predisposition to elimination and death – which is, properly speaking, sovereignty – was long ago forgotten by politicians (they are sometimes recalled to it by the involuntary sacrifice of their lives). Their sole objective remains the renewal of their class and its privileges(?) with our most total connivence, it must be said, which is justified by the fact that they are the perverse instrument of our sovereignty.

One always hopes that the politicians will admit their uselessness, their duplicity, their corruption. One is always on the look-out for an ultimate demystification of their sayings and doings. But could we bear this? For the politician is our mask, and if we tear it off we run the risk of ending up with our responsibility painfully exposed, that very responsibility we relinquished to the politician's advantage.

Corruption: that is, indeed, the heart of the problem.

It is never an accident. It is inherent in the exercise of power and, hence, in the exercise of evil. The whole world over and wherever they come from, those who reach the nerve centre of affairs are immediately transfigured by corruption and it is here that their real complicity is forged.

But the complicity does not end there – nor the essence of evil.

For the corruption of the élites is, precisely, the corruption of everyone: corruption is a collective psychodrama and, since we have the leaders we deserve, if we feel contempt for them it is only ever the reflection of the contempt we each feel for ourselves as political animals.

Doubtless we should even see corruption as one of the real rules of the game, the echo of a basic symbolic rule (different from politics and the social), which has become, above and beyond all morality, a practical, immanent and secret rule of operation. A serious question this, since it concerns the whole of public morality and connects with Mandeville's hypothesis on the supremacy of vice in the happy conduct of affairs.

The corruption of ideas is no exception.

They too follow a much more cynical, subtle trajectory than the pathways of reason, and the networks of thought that are created bear only a distant relation to truth.

It is this cunning which means that, as soon as they are invested with power, politicians immediately turn against that which, or those who, carried them to power, just as intellectuals very quickly turn against the very ideas that inspired them.

There is no point, then, tormenting oneself over this state of corruption, in which is to be seen the radicality of politics – or, in other words, from which we can read off what politics is in its symbolic dimension: namely, a sharing-out of evil.

Such is the living coin of power in a confrontation that goes way beyond representation, in a system of obligation in which there is always a gift and a counter-gift, a lethal revenge.

This is the 'two-sidedness of corruption'. Where those in power are concerned, the aim is to corrupt the dominated, to induce in them some form or other of 'voluntary servitude'. Whereas the aim of the dominated is to corrupt the dominant precisely by their voluntary servitude, which they turn round against them like a weapon: this is the whole strategy of the masses, of the silent majorities.

Once the great and the good had the privilege of granting pardon. Today, they want to be pardoned in their turn. They take the view that, on the basis of human rights, they are entitled to the universal compassion that had until now been the prerogative of the poor and of victims (in fact we cannot pardon them enough and they deserve all our compassion, not for reasons of rights or morality, but quite simply because there is nothing worse than being in power).

However this may be, they believe they must now stand before the moral tribunal of public opinion and even declare their corruption before it (more or less spontaneously!). They would even accuse themselves of crimes they did not commit in order to gain an artificial immunity as a by-product.

But the cunning of the dominated is even subtler.

If consists not in pardoning them (you do not pardon those in power), nor in inflicting any real punishment on them, but in passing over their little acts of embezzlement and this faked-up spectacle with a certain indifference. And this should leave the politicians very crestfallen, as it is the clear sign of their insignificance for everyone. Some of them have demanded to be judged and found guilty (though they are innocent, of course!). But the 'ordeal' the judges have put the politicians and the big industrialists through has in the end only restored legitimacy, recognition and an audience to people who had lost them.

Hence the strange confusion that prevails in the political sphere. For there is in the fact of this universal compassion a deep disturbance of symbolic regulation. Everywhere today we see the tormentors (pretending to) take the victim's side, showing them compassion and compensating them (as in Charles Najman's film *La mémoire est-elle soluble dans l'eau...?*). This may perhaps resolve things on the moral plane, but it aggravates them at the symbolic level.

On the symbolic plane there is only one way to pay back, and that is the counter-gift. If that is impossible, then there is vengeance, which is itself a form of counter-gift. Compassion here is useless and perverse: it merely adds to the inferiority of the victim.

Moreover, this ruse of repentance is a particularly underhand manoeuvre on the part of those in power, since it means stealing from the people the last of their rights, their only opportunity for political participation: the chance to unmask and condemn the powerful.

It is the same with the media and the news sources when they put themselves in the dock and engage in self-criticism. They rob the public of the last of their rights as citizens – the right not to believe a single word they are told.

Just as advertising, by affecting a self-deprecating ironic tone, short-circuits our opportunities for deriding it. This kind of deterrence is at work everywhere: 'citizens' are deprived of their right of revenge and their capacity to take reprisals.

Happily, the citizen still has the spectacle and the ironic enjoyment of that spectacle. For, if we are politically under house arrest, and if we cannot be the actors of politics, we must at least have the spectacle of politics. It was already like this, according to Rivarol, during the French Revolution: the people did not mind making revolution, but primarily they wanted the spectacle of revolution.

Here again, then, it is naïve to pity those populations that are condemned to 'the society of the spectacle'. Alienated they may be, but their servitude is double-edged. And there is here, in this combination of indifference and the enjoyment of politics as spectacle, a mischievous form of revenge.

The Destruction of the Golden Temple

There is no longer any metaphysical presence of evil nowadays, no presence of God or the Devil who fought above our heads and did battle over our souls.

There is no longer any mythological presence of evil, the presence of a Mephisto or a Frankenstein embodying its principle.

Our evil is faceless and imageless. It is present everywhere in homeopathic doses, in the abstract patterns of technology, but it no longer has any mythic presence.

There remains, however, some spark of evil in the heart of modern industrial misfortune – perhaps not evil in the pure state, but a little spark of it all the same – as, for example, in the Villa Palagonia in the heart of Palermo's suburbs where happiness and misfortune are conjured away simultaneously by a truly evil piece of stage-management – that of all the distorting mirrors her lover sets up around her – around his wife's beauty – to entrap her.

Or in the fabulous story of *The Temple of the Golden Pavilion* told by Yukio Mishima:

> This beautiful building was before long going to be turned into ashes, I thought. As a result, my image of the Golden Temple gradually came to be superimposed on the real temple itself in all its details...: the roof in my image was superimposed on the real roof. ... The Golden Temple ... had, so to speak, been

transformed into a symbol of the real world's evanescence. Owing to this process of thought, the real temple had now become no less beautiful than that of my mental image. Tomorrow, for all we knew, fire might rain down from the sky. ... But for the present it stood serenely before us in all its fine details, bathing in that light which was like the summer's fire.[31]

The courage required to make a confession was a trifling matter. ... The fact is that by ... refusing to confess I had until then been experimenting with the single problem: 'Is evil possible?' If I were to persist until the end in not confessing, it would prove that evil, albeit merely a petty evil, was indeed possible. ... The thought that if I should confess, the first petty evil of my life would collapse, held me back.[32]

Good wants always to speak itself, whereas evil is bound up with secrecy. Hence the confession of sex and, before long, simply the frenzied urge to talk of it. The parading of sex, from the obnoxious to innocuousness; cleansing and absolution by language. The special quality of hell is to see everything clearly down to the last detail.[33]

On the one hand, a phantasm of immortality emerged from the apparently destructible aspect of human beings; on the other, the apparently indestructible beauty of the Golden Temple gave rise to the possibility of destroying it. Mortal things like human beings cannot be eradicated; indestructible things like the Golden Temple can be destroyed. ... If I were to set fire to the Golden Temple... I should be committing an act of

31. Yukio Mishima, *The Temple of the Golden Pavilion*. Translated by Ivan Morris (London: Vintage, 2001), pp. 41–2.
32. Ibid. pp. 82–3.
33. Ibid., p. 95. The passage in italics doesn't appear in the current French edition of Mishima's work or in the English translation.

pure destruction, of irreparable ruin, an act which would truly decrease the volume of beauty that human beings had created in this world.[34]

Nothing else can change anything in this world. Knowledge alone is capable of transforming the world, while at the same time leaving it exactly as it is. When you look at the world with knowledge, you realize that things are unchangeable and at the same time are constantly being transformed. You may ask what good it does us. Let's put it this way – human beings possess the weapon of knowledge in order to make life bearable. For animals such things aren't necessary. Animals don't need knowledge or anything of the sort to make life bearable. But human beings do need something, and with knowledge they can make the very intolerableness of life a weapon, though at the same time that intolerableness is not reduced in the slightest.

...Well, beauty – beauty that you love so much – is an illusion of the remaining part, the excessive part, which has been consigned to knowledge. It is an illusion of the 'other way to bear life' which you mentioned.[35]

If I burn down the Golden Temple, I told myself, I shall be doing something that will have great educational value. For it will teach people that it is meaningless to infer indestructibility by analogy. They will learn that the mere fact of the Golden Temple's having continued to exist, of its having continued to stand for five hundred and fifty years by the Kyoko Pond, confers no guaranty upon it whatsoever. They will be imbued with a sense of uneasiness as they realize that the self-evident

34. Ibid., pp. 182–3. The term translated here as phantasm is rendered as 'simulacre' in the French.
35. Ibid., pp. 203–4. The term translated as 'illusion' here is rendered in the French as 'fantôme'.

175

axiom which our survival has predicated on the temple can collapse from one day to another.

The continuity of our lives is preserved by being surrounded by the solidified substance of time. . . . Take, for example, a small drawer, which the carpenter has made for the convenience of some household. With the passage of time, the actual form of this drawer is surpassed by time itself and, after the decades and centuries have elapsed, it is as though time had become solidified and had assumed that form. A given small space, which was at first occupied by the object, is now occupied by solidified time. It has in fact become the incarnation of a certain form of spirit. . . . It is written . . . that after a hundred years have passed and objects have been transformed into spirits, the hearts of men are deceived, and this is given the name of Tsukumogami, the year of the mournful spirit. It is the custom of the world to remove one's old household utensils each year before the advent of Spring and to throw them into the alley; and this is known as the house-sweeping.[36]

Thus my deed would open the eyes of men to the disasters of the Tsukumogami and save them from those disasters. By my deed I should thrust the world in which the Golden Temple existed into a world where it did not exist. The meaning of the world would surely change.[37]

It is a truly superb allegory, this story of the Golden Temple: the allegory of evil's revenge, of destruction as the only way out from beauty and the excess of beauty.

But not just beauty. Evil can also befall intelligence.

Intelligence protects us from nothing – not even from stupidity.

36. Ibid., pp. 183–4
37. Ibid., p. 184.

Being intelligent is not enough, then, to prevent one from being stupid, and sometimes intelligence even lives in stupidity's shade, and vice versa.

Not only does intelligence not mark the end of stupidity, there is no other way out from excess of intelligence but stupidity. In keeping with an implacable reversibility, stupidity lies in wait for it, as its shadow, as its double.

Only thought, only lucidity, which stands as much opposed to intelligence as to stupidity, can escape this trial of strength.

But there is no rule, no more for good than for evil: they chase each other endlessly around the Moebius strip.

Given the hellish production of collective intelligence, we shall have to reckon in the future with an ever-higher rate of artificial stupidity.

A few millennia further down the road of the last century – and everything men do will exhibit the highest intelligence; but that way intelligence will have lost all its dignity. By then it will doubtless be necessary to be intelligent, but it will also be so common and vulgar that a nobler taste will experience this necessity as a *vulgarity*. And just as a tyranny of truth and science could make lying more highly esteemed, a tyranny of intelligence would be capable of producing a new species of nobility. To be noble might then come to mean: to have madness in one's head.'[38]

38. Nietzsche, *Die fröhliche Wissenschaft*, Book 1, Section 20. I have used my own translation here, as Baudrillard's French version differs considerably from the available English ones. In particular, the term *Klugheit* is rendered here as 'intelligence', where Walter Kaufmann, for example, translates as 'prudence'. And where some English translations work from a text containing the phrase 'ein eklerer Geschmack', this French version clearly assumes 'ein edlerer Geschmack', which seems rather more probable.

With the emergence of Artificial Intelligence – the 'highest stage of intelligence', that of an integral, limitless intelligence – it will not even have taken thousands of years for Nietzsche's prophecy to come true.

An asexual intelligence, unfolding by contiguity and brain-grafting. A fractal intelligence and yet an intelligence undivided since, though subdividing indefinitely, it is never opposed to itself.

An absolute progress, then, towards the ramification of single-cell organisms, towards a numerical sequencing and automatic calculation anterior to any complex, analytical thought. The mental equivalent of biological regression to a stage prior to that of sexuation: the genetic involution of the species towards the zero degree of procreation in cloning parallels the mental involution of the species towards the zero degree of thought in Artificial Intelligence.

It seems nothing can counteract the proliferation of this Artificial Intelligence based on the zero degree of thought.

Nothing, that is, except this reversibility of intelligence and stupidity – the latter representing a renewed challenge to victorious intelligence.

There is something here too like a revenge of evil.

Something to which the tyranny of reality leads equally well – to appreciating any old form of madness and illusion.

What the tyranny of Artifical Intelligence leads to most surely is the birth of a previously unknown stupidity – artificial stupidity – deployed everywhere on the screens and in the computer networks. It is at this point that natural stupidity may, like madness, recover a degree of nobility in abreaction to Integral Reality.

When intelligence becomes hegemonic, becoming a mode of technical, collective, automatic adaptation, then any other hypothesis than intelligence becomes preferable. Stupidity becomes preferable.

When the hypothesis of intelligence ceases to be *sovereign* and becomes *dominant*, then it is the hypothesis of stupidity that becomes sovereign. A stupidity that might be said to be a sort of higher intelligence, on the verge of a radical thought – that is to say, beyond truth.

Artificial Intelligence, for its part, sees itself as purged of all stupidity; it prefers to overlook the eternal duel between intelligence and stupidity – it is in this sense that it is stupid: it is like a disembodied thought that could be said to have lost its shadow. Now, he who has lost his shadow is merely the shadow of himself.

At any rate, no one knows what the destiny of this intelligence will be.

Perhaps natural selection will win out even among artificial entities.

Every day thousands of sites die out on the Internet. What applied in the case of living beings over the course of evolution is continuing now in that of digital, genetic, cybernetic artefacts, doomed to disappear in droves to leave only a few of them, or their distant descendants along the digital chain. And we are only at the dawn of this ruthless selection process. In the order of artificial beings, we are at the stage occupied by bacteria in the order of life.

'The measurement of intelligence,' says Stephen Jay Gould, 'is itself the mark of unintelligence.'

In the symbolic chain, nothing is comparable with anything else; there is no scale of measurement. Man and animals and the other forms are part of a chain, but do not merge with each other.

It is when they are 'liberated', unchained from each other, that they become comparable, measurable and almost automatically inferior or superior to one another. All hierarchies, discriminations and scales of superiority derive from this passage through comparability, measurement and the ideological instruments of measurement. The measurement of IQ is simply the caricatural example.

Why do we persist in measuring intelligence? If it exists, it does so in the much more subtle sense of complicity (intelligence with the enemy!). And, in that sense, anyone 'at the bottom of the scale' can have greater intelligence than anyone else at the top.

By contrast with the exponential character of technical and digital intelligence and the virtually infinite expansion of the networks, thought is finite.

By its very singularity it remains a circumscribed, initiatory form.

It will never be available at will by a mere productive miracle, such as the one flooding the market of knowledge, information and skills.

Understood as empirical, mechanical functioning, there is, according to the whole of modern analytic philosophy (Turing), a highest stage of the machine, of mathematical calculation and technicity in general.

Moreover, this analytic function has a history, whereas thought does not (Adorno: 'No universal history leads from savagery to humanitarianism, but there is one leading from the slingshot to the megaton bomb'[39]).

---

39. *Negative Dialectics.* Translated by E. B. Ashton (London, Routledge, 1973), p. 320.

Thought is finite, technical intelligence is infinite. It presupposes an irreversible evolution, a highest stage which Turing glimpsed as a definitive ideal.

Thought is measured by a different rule, and puts us in mind, rather, of those souls whose number, according to certain ancient myths, is limited.

There was in that time a limited contingent of souls or spiritual substance, redistributed from one living creature to the next as successive deaths occurred. With the result that some bodies were sometimes waiting for a soul (like present-day heart patients waiting for an organ donor).

On this hypothesis, it is clear that the more human beings there are, the rarer will be those who have a soul. Not a very democratic situation and one which might be translated today into: the more intelligent beings there are (and, by the grace of information technology, they are virtually all intelligent), the rarer thought will be.

Christianity was first to institute a kind of democracy and generalized right to a personal soul (it wavered for a long time where women were concerned). The production of souls increased substantially as a result, like the production of banknotes in an inflationary period, and the concept of soul was greatly devalued. It no longer really has any currency today and it has ceased to be traded on the exchanges.

There are too many souls on the market today. That is to say, recycling the metaphor, there is too much information, too much meaning, too much immaterial data for the bodies that are left, too much grey matter for the living substance that remains. To the point where the situation is no longer that of bodies in search of a soul, as in the archaic liturgies, but of innumerable souls in search of a body. Or an incalculable knowledge in search of a knowing subject.

Such is our intelligence, that intelligence that lives on the illusion of an exponential growth of our stock.

Whereas the most probable hypothesis is that the human race merely has at its disposal, today, as it had yesterday, a general fund, a limited stock that redistributes itself across the generations, but is always of equal quantity.

In intelligence, we might be said to be infinitely superior, but in thought we are probably exactly the equal of preceding and future generations.

There is no privilege of one period over another, nor any absolute progress – there, at least, no inequalities. At species level, democracy rules.

This hypothesis excludes any triumphant evolutionism and also spares us all the apocalyptic views on the loss of the 'symbolic capital' of the species (these are the two standpoints of humanism: triumphant or depressed). For if the original stock of souls, natural intelligence or thought at humanity's disposal is limited, it is also indestructible. There will be as much genius, originality and invention in future periods as in our own, but not more – neither more nor less than in former ages.

This runs counter to two perspectives that are corollaries of each other: positive illuminism – the euphoria of Artificial Intelligence – and regressive nihilism – moral and cultural depression.

All this arises from the fact that, though we have a purchase on intelligence, and a purchase on the world by way of intelligence, thought, for its part, does not depend on us. It comes to us from the world, which thinks us.

The world is not intelligent, but thought has nothing to do with intelligence. The world is not what we think, it is what thinks us in return.

[I]f one did not look at the world with the world's eyes, the world already in one's own gaze, it fell apart into meaningless details that live as sadly far apart from each other as the stars in the night-sky.

Robert Musil

The 'Blowback' of Duality

Our entire system, both technical and mental, tends towards oneness, identity and totality, at the cost of an extraordinary simplification. And the whole of our metaphysics and all our neuroses chart the evils and confusions that ensue from that simplification.

But duality is indefectible.

It is totality that falters in the more or less long term.

Any political, economic, moral or mental system that achieves this even virtual totalization, that achieves this kind of perfection, either automatically fractures or duplicates itself to infinity in a simulacrum of itself. Everything that comes close to its definitive formula or its absolute potency can only repeat itself indefinitely or produce a monstrous double – whether it be terrorism or clones.

There is never any equilibrium state or state of completion that cannot suddenly be destabilized by a process of automatic reversion.

Everything which offends against duality, which is the fundamental rule, everything which aims to be integral, leads to disintegration through the violent resurgence of duality – or in conformity with the principle of evil, whichever you prefer.

It is duality and reversibility which everywhere govern the principle of evil. It is duality, liquidated everywhere, conjured away by all possible means, that restores an absence and an emptiness that are generally submerged by a total presence. It is duality that fractures Integral Reality, that smashes every unitary or totalitarian system by emptiness, crashes, viruses or terrorism.

A reversibility that can be seen even in natural catastrophes which intervene in the course of the world with consummate indifference, which explains why they exert a profound fascination. This is also the charm of the weather; insofar as it is unpredictable, it continues to terrify, and to fuel, the imagination.

So it is with the smallest earthquake, the least accident, some terrorist act or other: these are all equivalent in the emergence of evil, in evil showing through like an inalienable dimension, irreducible to the rational order.

There is no point deploring this – nor exalting it for that matter. These are quite simply the rules of the game. Every-thing that seeks to infringe these rules, to restore a universal order, is a fraud.

Our moral law is one of universal rationalization, of re-totalization of the universe according to the law. But the moral law can do nothing against the rules of the game and the order of evil, which takes its revenge come what may.

Everything turns around. And the virtual completion of the world, the perfect crime, the fantastic attempt to bring into being an integral world – that phantasm of total information paradoxically allows us to glimpse an even more fundamental form: that of its radical incompletion.

In the same way, Integral Reality brings the spectre of radical illusion into view, or back into view.

The height of obscenity brings the re-emergence of the pattern of seduction: 'What are you doing after the orgy?'[40]

So it is that Artificial Intelligence opens on to the radical exercise of thought. So it is that the paroxysm of technology opens on to the constellation of the mystery (Heidegger[41]). There is a kind of predestination in this.

This reversibility means that the object and the subject are in a sense predestined. So it is with the feminine and the masculine in seduction: they become each other's destiny instead of remaining face to face in the mirror of alienation.

There is no equivalent in terms of which they could be exchanged, short of taking sex, sexuality, as a kind of general equivalent, which we do, in fact, do today in reducing masculine and feminine to their 'difference'.

Similarly, we reduce life and death to the opposition between them, reduce them to opposing terms or, in other words, to their 'objective' reality. Now, neither life nor death can be exchanged for anything.

There is no equivalence in the name of which they could be exchanged.

They alternate and that is all there is to it. Like the seasons, like the elements that change into one another – fire, water, earth and air. Like colours: neither red nor blue can be exchanged; they are exchanged only in terms of wavelength. Otherwise, they are incomparable qualities.

40. This phrase is in English in the original.
41. Baudrillard writes 'la constellation du secret' here, quoting Heidegger in the standard French translation by André Préau, which reads 'la constellation, le mouvement stellaire du secret'. 'La question de la technique', *Essais et conférences*, Paris: Gallimard, 1958, p. 45. William Lovitt renders this as 'the constellation, the stellar course of the mystery'. *The Question Concerning Technology and Other Essays* (New York: Harper & Row, 1977), p. 33.

Or, rather, there is a duel between them: death toys with life, life toys with death.

Which of the two succumbs?

Stanislaw Lec reverses the terms here: it is not we who defend ourselves against death, it is death that defends itself against us: 'Death resists us, but it gives in in the end.'

Nothing else so stunning as this has ever been said about death.

Needless to say, this dual relationship has nothing to do with interactivity, which is a parody of it. There is nothing interactive in the antagonistic process of reversibility and becoming.

The feminine and the masculine are not 'interactive': that is ridiculous.

Life and the world are not interactive – life isn't a question-and-answer session or a video game.

There is nothing interactive in words when they are articulated in language.

Interactivity is a gigantic mythology, a mythology of integrated systems or of systems craving integration, a mythology in which otherness is lost in feedback, interlocution and interface – a kind of generalized echography.

Nor is there any interface between gods and men.

The only rule, as everywhere else, is the dual rule of gift and counter-gift.

According to Bataille, we live on the immense free gift of solar energy, on that natural excess and unreciprocated prodigality. But there is no natural excess and the sun does not dispense its energy free of charge. The Aztecs knew this, they who made it function by performing human sacrifices. Solar energy itself is the product of a dual, sacrificial exchange, a real potlatch. You sacrifice to the gods and they sacrifice in return to make the light exist and with it the stars and living creatures. Or the gods sacrifice themselves first and human beings reciprocate: the dual form plays in both directions.

What would humans be if the sun afforded them its light with nothing in return? If they are not able to give anything back, they are nothing. Conversely, if the gods did not respond to human sacrifice with their blessings they would be nothing. They would not even exist.

Nothing has existence in itself. Nothing exists except in dual, antagonistic exchange.

We have put an end to this dual relation with the sun.

With nuclear power and the bomb, says Canetti in a superb image, we have annexed the sun; we have dashed it down on to the earth, without any possibility of surrendering it, and its light then is a light of death.

Reversibility is still there, but it takes the form of vengeance.

Lines of Fracture

Lines of fracture, inversions, splits, rifts: there is, as it were, a line beyond which, for every expanding system – every system which, by dint of exponential growth, passes beyond its own end – a catastrophe looms.

We are no longer in a system of growth, but of excrescence and saturation, which can be summed up in the fact that there is too much.

There is too much everywhere, and the system cracks up from excess.

Every mass produces a critical mass effect – in the physical sense of a certain magnitude (mass, temperature, pressure) that produces a radical change in the properties of a body or in the development of a phenomenon.

It is in this way that every phenomenon can reverse its course by mere acceleration or proliferation. It is in this way that a simple variation in the overall mass of the cosmos can tip our universe over from expansion to sudden, violent contraction.

All velocity produces an equivalent or even greater mass.

All acceleration produces an equal or even greater inertia.

All mobilization produces an equal or even greater immobility.

All differentiation produces an equal or even greater indifference.

All transparency produces an equal or even greater opacity.

All information produces an equal or even greater entropy or disinformation.

All communication produces an equal or even greater incommunicability.

All knowledge, all certainty produces an equal or even greater uncertainty.

Etc.

Every process growing exponentially generates a barrier: the speed barrier, the heat barrier, the information barrier, the transparency barrier, the Virtual barrier. And that barrier is insuperable.

The energy of acceleration is exhausted in compensating for the inertia resulting from that acceleration.

The additional information intended to offset the perverse effects of information merely reinforces those effects.

Every exponential form leads to the critical threshold at which the process reverses its effects.

For example, the accumulation of truth, of the signs of truth, produces an irresistible effect of uncertainty.

There is nothing more dissuasive than the accumulation of evidence.

Nothing more unreal than the accumulation of facts.

On the horizon of the signs of the real the simulacrum looms.

When the signs of good accumulate, the era of evil and the transparency of evil begins.

In this way, the passage from the true to the false (or rather to the undecidable), from the real to the simulacrum, from good to evil, is like a critical mass effect, a non-dialectical logic, a fateful logic of excess.

The excess of health engenders viruses and virulence.

The excess of security produces a new threat, that of immune system failure.

The excess of capital engenders speculation and financial collapse.

The excess of information engenders undecidability of facts and confusion of minds.

The excess of reason engenders the unjustifiable.

The excess of transparency engenders terror.

The gravitational collapse of every system, of every process, of every body in movement, whose acceleration creates a reciprocal shock wave, an antagonistic force not just equal but greater, which constitutes its absolute limit, its negative horizon, and beyond which it cancels itself out.

Too much is too much.

Without noticing it, we have gone through the social barrier, the politics barrier, the information barrier. It might even be said that we have gone through the virtual reality barrier and we are approaching the critical eventuality of a collapse of the information systems.

Perhaps, like demographic growth, intelligence itself, in its neuronal extension, constitutes a critical mass?

There will soon be as many artificial neurones on earth, in all of our 'intelligent' machines, as in all our 'natural' brains (120 billion neurones each). Are we not running the risk, after the elimination of dark matter,[42] of an exhaustion of all grey matter, from the point when the stock of Artificial Intelligence exceeds the symbolic capital of the species, this

42. I take this to be a reference to the recent challenges to conventional assumptions on the extent of dark matter in the universe. See, for example, the article 'Things Fall Apart' in *The Economist*, 5 February 2004.

latter ceasing to exist once its much more efficient artificial counterpart comes into being?

Is there room on the earth for as many artificial as natural species, for as much computer-generated substance as organic matter, dead or alive, for as much Artificial Intelligence as natural intelligence?

Is there room for both the world and its double?

So long as we were in a kind of spatial, geographical and mental infinity and transcendence, universality could function as a dynamic idea – totality being fine and desirable only as a dream.

What we have today is the absolute reverse of the dialectic of the universal, the stage of the globalization of a finite, excessive, transcendence-less universe.

Too much is too much.

The 'fine souls' say: 'The excess of culture will never abolish the desire for culture. The profusion of sex will never abolish desire.'

And the same goes for communication, information, democracy and human rights too. They cannot imagine that there is too much (yet obesity, that surfeit of body-mass, ought to make them think).

All this is wrongheaded. Nothing escapes the law of sudden, violent deflation through excess, through overproduction – particularly not desire, which is pretty much geared to lack!

The same law applies here as in the markets, and the same crash looms over any form of excrescence, be it sexual, cultural or economic.

Information, communication, production, spectacle – what if there were an explosive accumulation of all these things?

We might think that the human capacity for adapting to the very worst is infinite. Most of the time it is proven to be so, and that can even produce an inverted thrill – but perhaps it will not turn out to apply indefinitely?

The surfeit of the social drives us out of the social.
The surfeit of politics drives us out of politics.
The surfeit of reality drives us out of reality.
One soul more and everywhere is overpopulated.[43]
One single element more and the whole system tips over into excess or exclusion.
A single mad cow and the whole herd has to be slaughtered.
This is the dictatorship of abundance, of excess, of the critical mass that overturns the accounting principles and sets us on an abusive, exponential course.

In any event, for the maleficent spirit of pataphysics everything is already excessive. The world itself is *de trop*.
The world, having become integral, absorbs everything into its fullness and, in so doing, expels itself. In its very totality, which is at once, like Ubu, naïve and ridiculous, it demonstrates irrational behaviour.
This is why, from a certain critical density onward (for example, the density of traffic in traffic jams), rational behaviour no longer pays. To move towards one's goal randomly is as efficient as taking a calculated route (as in Naples, for example, where absolute disorder produces the same results as absolute order).
Sometimes irrational behaviour can even be superior to the rational: so, for example, two boats on Lake Constance

---

43. 'Un seul être de plus et tout est surpeuplé.' This echoes Lamartine's famous line from the seventh stanza of 'L'isolement' (*Méditations*): 'Un seul être vous manque et tout est dépeuplé.' Interestingly, this line was also parodied by Jean Giraudoux in *La Guerre de Troie n'aura pas lieu* as 'Un seul être vous manque et tout est repeuplé.'

in dense fog are in less danger of colliding if their pilots are drunk than if they are attempting to master the situation.

And from this we can draw some conclusions regarding the beneficial effect of evil and also the diabolic effect of good.

In our current situation, where we are everywhere on the verge of this critical density, if not indeed beyond it, the wise thing would be to act generally in irrational ways. Out of intolerance to the system itself.

For, paradoxically, whereas tolerance is held up everywhere as the supreme value, the question of intolerance to the system itself and to its effects is never raised, of intolerance to good and to the excess of good.

Tolerance, this peaceful coexistence of all cultures, all religions, of mores and ideas, is more or less the equivalent of that degraded form of energy that is heat (leaving aside the fact that, following its own 'humanitarian' logic, it assumes, on occasion, entirely intolerant forms of intervention).

In a world ruthlessly doomed to this principle, the irruption of intolerance will soon be the only event. The automatic return of all forms of racism, integrism and exclusion in reaction to this unconditional conviviality.

Whereby evil ironically resurfaces.

However, it may seem that positive values emerge from evil, but once again it is evil that is at work in this ironic reversal – there is, once again, in this violation of logic a violence done to reason.

It was in this way that Jarry drew happy consequences from the exponentiality of sex, writing in *The Supermale* that once a certain critical threshold has been passed, you can make love indefinitely...

But that is pataphysics!

Parallel Universes

The totalization of the world, this coming of an Integral Reality, leaves behind it all kinds of useless functions: the body, sex, reproduction, language, death. All this is useless from the viewpoint of the networks, of cloning and of Artificial Intelligence. Thought, work and the real, voided of their essence by their substitutes, become relics or useless oddities.

Death itself ceases to be an event, a specific, individual destiny. Diluted in the clone or in a kind of mental coma, it disappears on the biological horizon of the machine body.

But perhaps it then becomes an inalienable singularity that assumes its full force as symbolic stake, as challenge, as pure form of reversibility?

Perhaps all these functions, at the same time as they disappear on the horizon of the real, are doomed to perpetuate themselves as parallel universes, as autonomous singularities, entirely dissociated from the dominant universe?

In this way, life itself can become a kind of parallel universe, something strange that happens to us while we are doing other things.

And the ego itself, freed from its identity, can strike out along the parallel paths of becoming.

Words, freed from their meanings, move on another orbit, that of language in the pure state.

In this way, starting out from what is expelled by the real, all sorts of silent circulations form – dual lives, absent events, transverse dimensions.

Existential Divide[44]

Birth as watershed, as demarcation line between two universes, the ego and the non-ego, the only potentiality that has been embodied being the ego.

But this differentiation is not as decisive as one thinks, as all the possibilities set aside at birth continue to run parallel to the ego, to the only potentiality realized, and from time to time make a foray into its lifeline.

It is these excluded alternatives that make up alterity and thereby one of the forms of becoming – linked to the possibility of crossing the line in the other direction, of going across that demarcation line towards the other, towards all the others – to become the other.

Whereas the ego of identity is content to pursue its history inside this lifeline, the play of destiny implies the crossing of this 'existential divide'.

Such are the two parallel dimensions of any existence: that of its history and its visible unfolding, and that of its becoming, a transfusion of forms towards these parallel universes, a devolution, an anamorphosis of the will.

Double life entails the notion of double death.

In one of these two lives you may already be dead, doubtless without knowing it. Sometimes it is the dead element that

---

44. 'Existential Divide', 'Time Divide' and 'Continental Divide' are in English in the original.

pulls the living along. In faces even, often one part is alive and the other already dead.

A double life entitles you to two deaths – and why not two amorous passions at the same time? So long as they remain parallel, all is well. It is when their paths cross that the danger arises. You may from time to time desert your life – one of the two – and take refuge in the other. The one in which you exist, the other in which you don't.

Where this living death doesn't exist, life takes its place. Just as the person who loses his shadow becomes the shadow of himself.

('The shadow of himself' – that would be a fine title. With the subtitle: 'Memoirs of a double life'.)

All identity problems run up against this parallax of death – this parallel axis of death. And this is never anything other than the day of reckoning contemporaneous with our existence, lived simultaneously – which does not, therefore, await us at the end of life, but accompanies us faithfully and implacably in it.

But this is merely one particular case in the distribution of life and death.

One is dead in one's lifetime itself; multiple deaths accompany us, ghosts that are not necessarily hostile, and yet others, not dead enough, not dead long enough to make a corpse.

So in *The Piano* (by Jane Campion), Ada – or at least one of the Adas – remained at the bottom of the ocean, bound to the piano that had sunk, and the other got free and resurfaced into a past – or later – life.

At any rate, we have all already been dead before living, and we came out of it alive. We were dead before and we shall be dead again after.

We do lots of wondering about the time after our death, but, paradoxically, none about the time before our birth.

Death and life can reverse themselves from this standpoint. And this implies another presence of death to life, because it – not simply an indeterminate nothingness, but a determinate, personal death – was there before and it does not cease to exist and to make itself felt with birth.

It is not merely hanging over the future like a sword of Damocles, it is also our prior destiny – there is something like a precession of death, which combines with the anticipation of the end in the very unfolding of our lives.

This connects up with the genetic process of apoptosis, in which the two opposing processes of life and death begin at the same time. In which death is not the gradual exhaustion of life: they are autonomous processes – complicit in a way, parallel and indissociable.

Hence the absurdity of wishing, as all our current technologies do, to eradicate death in favour of life alone.

Along these same lines of thinking, Lichtenberg made an amusing suggestion: he imagined a world in which human beings would be born in old age and would get younger and younger until they became children again – these latter continuing to get younger until they were put in bottles where, after returning to the embryonic state, they would lose their lives. 'Girls of fifty to sixty would find particular pleasure in raising their now tiny mothers in bottles...'

Time Divide

One can imagine also a temporal dividing line with time flowing off to either side of it, in accordance with a contradictory double arrow, like the waters separated by the Continental Divide that are in the end reunited in the same oceanic cycle.

According to Ilya Prigogine, we intuitively sense the irreversibility of physical phenomena and time's arrow is irreversible. But we may hypothesize a reversible process at the very heart of time, and at the very heart of thought. A dual arrow of time, a dual arrow of thought (according to some scientists, the elementary physical laws are reversible; that is to say, their mathematical expression is unchanged if the temporal variable is reversed). How can we reconcile this reversibility with the irreversibility we observe on the basis of the commonplace intuition we have of time?

This other dimension of time isn't another directional arrow in the opposite direction. It isn't a regression (as in most science fiction novels), but a reversion. And if we may designate the usual dimension of time with an arrow, then the other would, rather, be a deviation, a clinamen, an opposite declination.

Ultimately, the Big Bang and the Big Crunch are born at the same time. The one does not come at the end of the other (any more than death comes at the end of life) or succeed the other in a cosmic cycle. They occur simultaneously and unfold in parallel, but in opposite directions.

It is as though time were squinting – a metalepsis that leads it to mistake the effect for the cause, and causes things to unfold in the other direction or, better, in both directions at once, like that famous wind that blows in all directions.

There is no more linearity, end or irreversibility than there is an indefinite linear function. In the order of chaos all systems and all functions convulse, bend back and fold in on themselves in accordance with a logic that excludes any evolutionary theory (and the theory of time's arrow, just like the theory of entropy, is an evolutionary theory).

Thus, what is merely a hypothesis where physics is concerned is a striking metaphor for our own lives and history: on our scale, too, things turn around at every moment, there is involution at the same time as there is evolution. Things are not first there and then gradually exhausted; they vanish as they appear.

To the phantasm of an integral universe of information and communication there stands secretly opposed the desire for a universe made up entirely of elective affinities and unforeseeable coincidences.

The universe of chance, luck and play.

In which nothing happens accidentally, but things happen rather by an internal necessity, or by happy or unhappy convergence.

Nothing is left to statistical probability here; all is left to the open possibility that the event may occur. Now, *everything wants to occur* and it is we who stand in the way of this infinite possibility.

All these events are potentially there. The potentiality in question is that of things yearning to appear and it has an echo within us. It is from this that the certainty comes that something *must* happen. And the event is made up of all those which, simultaneously, did not take place. For nothing of what did not take place disappears entirely. Absent events continue to exist as part of a parallel history and at times re-emerge suddenly in a manner unintelligible to us. The actual present is made up of this ever-living inactuality.

John Updike, in *Toward the End of Time*:

'Perhaps': the word is like the little fork in reality when a quantum measurement is made. Each time that we measure either the position or momentum of an elementary particle, the other specific becomes, by Heisenberg's indeterminacy principle, unknowable. The 'wave function' of the particle collapses. Our universe is the one containing our observation. But, some cosmic theorists aver, the system – containing the particle, the measuring apparatus, and the observer – continues to exist in its other possible states, in parallel universes that have branched from this moment of measurement. The theory is called that of 'many worlds.' ... From the same verifiable quantum formulations arises the possibility that our universe, born from nothing, was instantly boosted, by the gravity-reversing properties of a 'false' vacuum, into an expansion so monstrous that the universe's real limits lie many times beyond the matter of which we can gather evidence with our farthest-seeing telescopes.[45]

The hypothesis of parallel events and lifelines throws into question the conception of linear, progressive history.

At any moment, the linear existence of the individual may be crossed by these lines of force from elsewhere. When these parallel lines never meet, it is a bad sign (but we do not live in a Euclidean geometry).

When nothing happens to interrupt the thread of history, then it can be regarded as dead, since it is unfolding in accordance with an identical model.

45. *Toward the End of Time* (London: Penguin. 1999), pp. 16–17.

We may mention here the concept of 'uchronia' introduced in the nineteenth century by the philosopher Renouvier, echoing the notion of utopia, but in the opposite direction.

Utopia relates to an imaginary future: 'What might happen ideally if...' Uchronia plays on this same standpoint, but with regard to the past: 'What might have happened if...' Bringing the variables around past events into play, what other event would we have ended up with? What other retrospectively possible sequence of events? (Take Cleopatra's nose, or the multiple random elements in the death of Diana or the unexpected arrival of Blücher on the battlefield at Waterloo...)

There is, thus, a whole uchronic 'imaginary', which we may regard as entirely futile if we take a realist view of things, but which assumes its full force if we retain the hypothesis of the potential force of absent events.

Today, utopia is at an end and uchronia with it. All these things have been absorbed into the only possible universe, that of real time and an inexorable present-ness.

At the same time as it gave rise to the utopian dimension, modernity gave rise to the opposite dimension of objective – technological, scientific, economic – reality, which relentlessly proceeds on its course to the exclusion of any imaginary order.

And if they were both able for a long while to lead contradictory, but collusive, existences, they have both been absorbed today into the operation of the Virtual.

In digital calculation, fiction can no longer resurface; as for the real, our good old real, which gloried in its image and its reference to the world – that disappeared long ago.

The possible itself is no longer possible.

What happens happens, and that's all there is to it.

It is the end of history, then, in its linear continuity and the end of the event in its radical discontinuity.

All that remains is the blatant self-evidence of actuality, of the actual performance, which, by that fact, becomes once again a total fiction and hallucination.

Anamnesis

It is probable that we have all been everywhere, in dreams, in an epileptic fit, in successive transmigrations and at present we are dying of boredom at always seeing the same places. Who can say with certainty whether he has or has not been to a particular place?

Guido Ceronetti

We have all been everywhere in some past life.

This suprasensory reminiscence, this 'journey of the soul' through places, bodies and successive lives, this fantasy ubiquity, has nothing to do with the ubiquity that is ours through the networks, through telepresence and telereality.

Though we might imagine the Virtual as the shortened version and prefigurement of future lives (not past ones any more), of a 'journey of the brain' (not the soul) through successive disembodiments – as the space-time of a spectral metempsychosis of the future.

The (radical) difference between virtual ubiquity and the anamorphosis of successive transmigrations is that in the space of the Virtual it is we who change place, who pass technologically from one place to another, whereas in the poetic space or in great mythology it is places, gods that metamorphose within us – and we are the theatre of that metamorphosis, the privileged site where their forces meet and where they all inhabit us, one by one, in some particular other life, at one moment or another.

Poetic man in Hölderlin's vision is like this: he is run through, shot through, by all divinities; he takes his source with all the rivers and inhabits all the mythic places of the globe, from Patmos to the Indus, by the mere force of becoming.

Becoming is linked to elementary forms, to natural or mythical beings or to all kinds of elective affinities by the same devolution, the same transference of will.

It is by paying this price that we pass from one form to the other, all of which can return. This is the secret meaning of the Eternal Return: all forms are both distinct and singular, but bound together in a chain. And if you manage to place yourself on this cycle of becoming, you can snake back endlessly from the one to the other and have control over them all.

This is what the gambler does in Paul Auster's *The Music of Chance*.

It is what the poem does when the sign become a destiny in which reality loses itself, when language becomes again the immense play of signs, the structuring of which escapes us...

The enumeration of rivers, mountains, gods, heroes, in the mythic unfolding of their births, their exploits, their sacrifices – and, ultimately, their mere naming.

The scattered elements of the poetic anagrammatization come together again in the pure utterance of the proper name. Naming cities, rivers, demigods, deified elements.

Melancthon Brunswick. Names, as fragments of a world out of joint, vestiges of a kind of cosmological disaster, but all speaking to each other across the ages, beyond history – no need even to recount any history.

An end to the sentimental panegyric of nature. Everything has become mythic – the seasons are there like gods, the rivers are there like gods.

There is also the infinite paradigm of language, the paradigm of the declension of cases: nominative, vocative, genitive, dative, but also active/passive, singular/dual. The noun (the name) alone, without attribute, without substance, without adjective, without verb, without complement, without history, bears the whole literal burden. The anagrammatization of all the names of God. And hence also his death, his perfect fragmentation, his end as transcendent totality.

Nietzsche, like Hölderlin, gives himself all the names of history, Dionysus, the Crucified one. He does not identify with them (that is madness), nor does he equate himself with them or measure himself against them (*hubris* and immoderation). He becomes all the Gods and Heroes and Rivers: anamorphosis, metamorphosis.

No metanoia or identification mania, but a chain of forms, figures, names.

Every name is a dual relation to the world, and each detail, each fragment, stands in a dual relation to the whole.

This is the fragment's revenge on the discourse.

The secret of the world is in the detail, in the fragment, in the aphorism – in the literal sense, *aphorizein* meaning to isolate, to separate, to cut off – not in the whole. It is through the detail that the anamorphosis, the metamorphosis of forms, passes, whereas the whole short-circuits this becoming by totalization of the meaning or the structure.

It is the same with Anagrams in language: the name of God is scattered through the poem; it now appears only fragmented, dismembered.

It will never be revealed.

It does not even become what it is, in keeping with the ensnaring formula of a finality of being; it simply *becomes*. That is to say, it passes from one form to the other, from one word to the other; it circulates in the detail of appearances.

Taken in its detail, the world is always perfectly self-evident.

Someone said: everything is true, nothing is exact.

I would say the opposite: nothing is true, everything is exact.

In this sense, any image, any act, any event, any detail of the world, is good, provided it is escribed, isolated, separated, scattered – anagrammatized, anamorphosed, 'aphoristic'.

The sign in general, as fragment, as particle wrested from the natural world, is already in itself an immediate subversion of the discourse of the real and of meaning in its pretension to totality.

Thought too must fragment and scatter.

Thought is a spectrum, and truth, if it exists, can only show through anagrammatically in the spectrum of thought.

'He could refract an idea which everyone thought simple into a hundred others, as the prism does with sunlight, each finer than the other, then gather together a host of others to re-create the white light of the sun, where others merely saw disorder and confusion' (Lichtenberg).

Rothko's transition to an immediate, definitive form, light years from what he was doing up to that point.

'My images have two characteristics: either they dilate and then open up in all directions, or they contract and then close up precipitately on all sides. Between these two poles lies everything I have to say.'

A change by which he separates himself miraculously from the artist he still was, with his place in the history of art, to be nothing but the sovereign medium of an extremely simple form, which no longer has anything to do with expressionism or abstraction.

'The form which appears stuns you with its simplicity. And perhaps the most surprising thing is that, during our earthly existence, in which our brains are bound with bands of steel – the tightly-fitting dream of our own personality – we have not peradventure given that little mental shake which would have freed the imprisoned thought and would have procured for it the ultimate intelligence' (Vladimir Nabokov).

Doesn't everyone have in them this potential change and becoming? This absolute singularity which demands only to occur effortlessly, an inspired form freed from the straitjacket of our individual being?
We have this becoming within us, and we lack nothing, since we are rid of truth.
The world too lacks nothing as it is; it opposes any attempt to make it signify anything whatever. To inflict truth on it is like explaining a joke or a funny story.

The poem too lacks nothing: any commentary makes it worse. Not only does it lack nothing, but it makes any other discourse appear superfluous.
Poetry and thought are to be taken in their literalness, not in their truth: truth merely makes things worse.

All language is *de trop*, except for the forms that know how to retain something of this silence and to set language off towards another destination – that of a shadow which follows us and unfolds beyond our presence.
In the anagrammaticality of poetic language, the words seem to have come from elsewhere, to have covered their

tracks, and yet to have been there forever. It seems that language, in its multiple singularity, has always been there. Better, it seems to be a long way ahead of us and to turn back in our direction to think us.

The singularity of a language is that, even if it has a history and an origin, it seems to reproduce itself 'as is' at every moment, and autonomously to re-invent itself. It is in this sense that we experience language as a kind of predestination – a kind of happy predestination.

The halting of becoming is the imposition of an end, of a finality, of any finality whatever.

The human race owes its becoming (and perhaps even its survival) entirely to the fact that it had no end in itself, and certainly not that of becoming what it is (of fulfilling itself, identifying with itself).

A fatal strategy that is perhaps itself coming to an end in our desperate effort to finalize the species at all costs, even in its genetic dimension, in order to enslave it to its own finality.

It is the same with the individual being. Its only chance of becoming is to have no end, no ideal formula or alternative solution.

Thought, too, while scattering its traces, leaves the literalness of the world intact, leaves intact the pure literalness of objects, though it sends their meaning up in smoke.

Shadowing the world[46] – following the word like its shadow to cover up its tracks and to show that, behind its supposed ends, it is going nowhere.

---

46. This phrase is in English in the original.

It is in this way that thought connects up with the event of the world – not with the occurrence of a totality that is nowhere to be found, but with the occurrence of the world as it is, in its unpredictable coming-to-pass.

It is in this way that we attain to the literalness, the material imagining, of the world, by the elimination of whatever obstacle may be between the image and the gaze.

The more daily life is eroded, routinized and interactivized, the more we must counter this trend with complex, initiatory sets of rules.

The more reality becomes reconciled with its concept in an objectless generality, the more we must seek out the initiatory rupture and the power of illusion.

If we cannot make the world the object of our desires, we can at least make it the object of a higher convention – which, precisely, eludes our desire.

Any illusion, any initiatory form, involves a severe rule.

Any created object, visual or analytic, conceptual or photographic, has to condense all the dimensions of the game into a single one: the allegorical, the representative (mimicry), the agonal (*agon*), the random (*alea*) and the vertiginous (*ilinx*).[47]

Recomposing the spectrum.

A work, an object, a piece of architecture, a photograph, but equally a crime or an event, must: be the allegory of something, be a challenge to someone, bring chance into play and produce vertigo.

47. These dimensions of play and games are identified in the work of Roger Caillois. See Caillois, *Man, Play and Games* (London, Thames and Hudson, 1962).